Official Cambridge Exam Preparation

OPEN WORLD

STRATEGY PLUS

B2 FIRST

INCLUSIVE WORKBOOK

with Audio

Claire Wijayatilake

with Jane Ritter

Cambridge University Press
www.cambridge.org/elt

Cambridge Assessment English
www.cambridgeenglish.org

Information on this title: www.cambridge.org/9781108727204

© Cambridge University Press and Cambridge Assessment 2021

First published 2021

20 19 18 17 16 15 14 13 12 11 10 9 8 7 6 5 4 3 2 1

Printed in Great Britain by CPI Group (UK) Ltd, Croydon CRO 4YY

A catalogue record for this publication is available from the British Library

ISBN 978-1-108-72720-4 Inclusive Workbook with Audio

CONTENTS

WELCOME TO OPEN WORLD

THE COURSE THAT TAKES YOU FURTHER

This workbook has the same aims and objectives as the original **Open World Workbook** in covering the course and preparing you for the exam. It is designed to give you further support both in the visual look and by giving additional help for exercises and tasks.

This workbook will also support you in thinking back to what you did in the Student's Book and will help you to look again at the language you learnt with clear links and other resources for the language covered.

It is important that you try the exercises first as this is the best way for you to learn. The support is there if you need it.

In the Starter Unit to Unit 7 there are exercises and tasks with a lot of additional support for you. From Unit 8 to Unit 14 you will notice you have less support, though there will still be support with strategies, as well as resources that link with the Student's Book. The aim is to help you focus on your learning to take you to the next level and to encourage you to make your own decisions in your learning.

LEARN ABOUT THE FEATURES IN YOUR NEW INCLUSIVE WORKBOOK

REMIND YOURSELF OF GRAMMAR STRUCTURES Scan the purple QR codes and watch the short grammar animations as many times as you want.

GRAMMAR BOXES Use the short presentation boxes to remind you of the grammar from the Student's Book and the grammar animations.

COLOUR CODING Helps you identify what to do in the task.

CLEAR LINKS SHOW YOU WHERE TO FIND EXTRA GRAMMAR HELP Try the exercises first, then use the links to the Grammar reference in the Student's Book if you need more help.

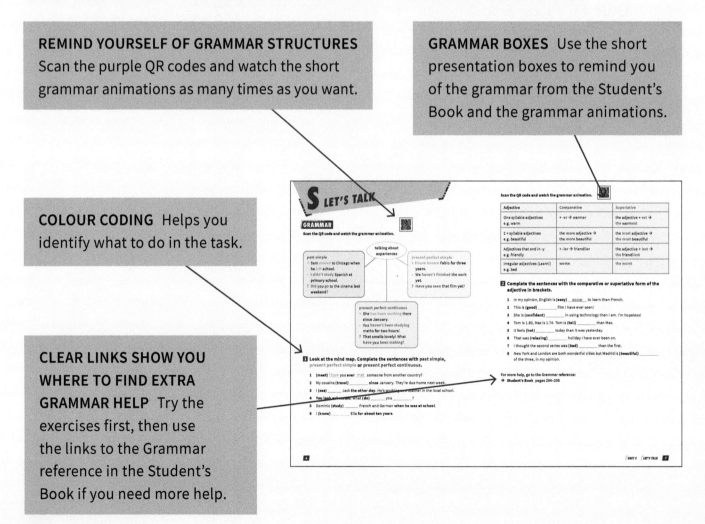

CLEAR LINKS SHOW YOU WHERE TO FIND VOCABULARY
Try the exercises first, then use the links to the Student's Book if you need more help.

STRATEGY
Read the tips and use different strategies to organise the task and help you complete it.

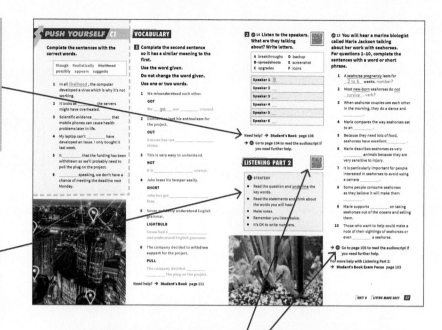

AUDIOSCRIPTS AT THE BACK OF THE BOOK
Scan the blue QR codes to listen to the task first, but if you want further support, use the audioscript to listen and read.

AUDIO OF READING TEXTS
Scan the orange QR code and listen to an audio recording of the text.

CLEAR LINKS SHOW YOU WHERE TO FIND MORE HELP WITH EXAM TASKS
Use the links to easily find more facts and tips about the exam tasks.

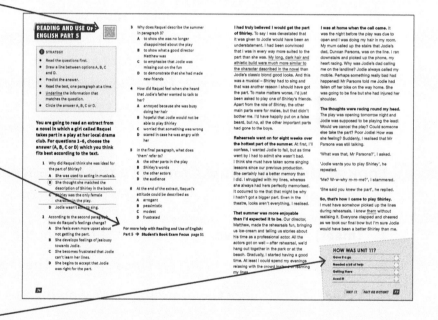

HOW WAS UNIT … ?
Think about the exercises in the unit and how much help you needed to do them.

This final section is to support you in thinking about what you have learnt and also how you managed to complete the exercises and tasks. As well as making your choice between **Gave it a go**, **Needed a bit of help**, **Getting there** and **Aced it!**, please think about why you made your choice from these four options. If you have not ticked **Aced it!** each time, think about what you did well, what you think you need to understand better, what further support you might need or what you can do yourself to get to **Aced it!** next time.

 LET'S TALK

GRAMMAR

Scan the QR code and watch the grammar animation.

talking about experiences

past simple
+ Sam moved to Chicago when he left school.
- I didn't study Spanish at primary school.
? Did you go to the cinema last weekend?

present perfect simple
+ I have known Fabio for three years.
- We haven't finished the work yet.
? Have you seen that film yet?

present perfect continuous
+ She has been working there since January.
- You haven't been studying maths for two hours!
? That smells lovely! What have you been making?

1 **Look at the mind map. Complete the sentences with past simple, present perfect simple or present perfect continuous.**

1 (meet) Have you **ever** met someone from another country?

2 My cousins (travel) _____ **since** January. They're due home next week.

3 I (see) _____ Jack **the other day**. He's working as a teacher in the local school.

4 **You look exhausted.** What (do) _____ you _____?

5 Dominic (study) _____ French and German **when he was at school**.

6 I (know) _____ Ella **for about ten years**.

6

Scan the QR code and watch the grammar animation.

Adjective	Comparative	Superlative
One syllable adjectives e.g. warm	+ -er → warmer	the adjective + est → the warmest
2 + syllable adjectives e.g. beautiful	the more adjective → the more beautiful	the most adjective → the most beautiful
Adjectives that end in -y e.g. friendly	+ -ier → friendlier	the adjective + iest → the friendliest
Irregular adjectives (Learn!) e.g. bad	worse	the worst

2 **Complete the sentences with the comparative or superlative form of the adjective in brackets.**

1   In my opinion, English is **(easy)** __easier__ to learn than French.

2   This is **(good)** _____ film I have ever seen!

3   She is **(confident)** _____ in using technology than I am. I'm hopeless!

4   Tom is 1.80, Max is 1.74. Tom is **(tall)** _____ than Max.

5   It feels **(hot)** _____ today than it was yesterday.

6   That was **(relaxing)** _____ holiday I have ever been on.

7   I thought the second series was **(bad)** _____ than the first.

8   New York and London are both wonderful cities but Madrid is **(beautiful)** _____ of the three, in my opinion.

For more help, go to the Grammar reference:
→ **Student's Book** pages 204–205

VOCABULARY

1 **Match the speakers (1–5) with the most appropriate adjective in the box.**

Write numbers.

delighted	1	annoyed	
worried		disappointed	
shocked			

1 I actually passed. I'm so happy because I worked really hard for these exams and now I can go to my first-choice university!

2 I've been waiting here for almost two hours. I'm now late for my next seminar and all I wanted to do was get a signature for this document.

3 Did you see the series finale?! I still can't believe how it ended. I really didn't see that coming, to be honest.

4 I'm really nervous about my driving test next week. I've practised a lot but I still don't think I'm ready for it.

5 I know I didn't do too well in the interview but I thought they might still offer me the job. It's sad but I will continue to apply for other roles.

Need help? ➔ **Student's Book** page 9

LISTENING

! STRATEGY

- Read each question and underline the key words.
- Draw lines between A–E.
- Note down some words you might hear.
- Listen carefully; use the script if necessary.

1 **🔊 02 You will hear five learners of English talking about difficulties they have with communication.**

For each speaker, choose a problem A–E.

A The speaker did the wrong kind of preparation for his/her overseas trip.

~~**B** The speaker's classmates were not interested in learning.~~

C The speaker lacked confidence because his/her English was not perfect.

D The speaker relied too heavily on translation from his/her mother tongue.

E The speaker mixes up different varieties of English.

Speaker 1	<u>B</u>
Speaker 2	___
Speaker 3	___
Speaker 4	___
Speaker 5	___

➔ 🔊 Go to page 96 to read the audioscript if you need further help.

WRITING

1 **Read this story about a girl called Anya.**

Complete the text with the correct words.

> secretly   On the bright side   ~~not even~~
> looking back   as you can imagine
> As long as   in theory

Two years ago, when I was 14, my parents decided to sign our family up for an experiment, which would be made into a reality TV series. What we would have to do is survive for a whole month without access to our usual communication devices. We would have no phones – **(1)** <u>not even</u> a landline – no radio, TV or computers. It was during the summer holidays so, **(2)** _____ , there was no reason why we couldn't live without those things – there was no homework to do for school. We could go to the local shop and we were allowed to buy a newspaper every day. Books were allowed, but not magazines.

I was not that keen on taking part but (3) _____ **I was hoping I would be talent-spotted and it would lead to a brilliant career in television.** My older brother, Marcus, was not that bothered as all he ever did was read books anyway. My sister, Molly, was too young to care. **(4)** _____ she had her toys and her pet rabbit to play with, she was fine. Mum and Dad were always telling me to 'get off that phone!' and they were the ones who applied to take part.

Anyway, (5) _____ **, it was quite a challenge for me!** I was so used to googling everything that came into my head, playing games on my phone for hours and chatting to my friends that being without technology was like losing part of my body. **(6)** _____ , the weather was great that summer so I spent a lot of time outside. I took up running and got really fit. I cycled over to my friends' houses as I couldn't call them to meet up in town. I read about five novels and really enjoyed the feel of an actual book in my hand. So, **(7)** _____ , it was not as bad as I had expected. Would I want to live like that all the time? Definitely not!

SPEAKING

1 🔊 03 **You will hear eight students answering a question.**

Listen and match speakers 1–6 to the questions they were asked A–F. Use different colours.

Speaker 1	A	What do you like about your hometown?
Speaker 2	B	When did you last go out with your friends?
Speaker 3	C	Which member of your family are you most similar to?

Speaker 4	D	Is there anyone in your family who inspires you?
Speaker 5	E	What sport or hobby would you like to try?
Speaker 6	F	Have you ever collected something?

➔ 🔊 Go to page 96 to read the audioscript if you need further help.

READING

1 **Read the article about artificial intelligence and language learning.**

> ⚠ **STRATEGY**
>
> - Read each question and <u>underline</u> the key words.
> - Look at the **bold** words in each paragraph.
> - <u>Underline</u> the words that give the answer.

1 As a language student, you have probably used artificial intelligence in numerous ways. You may have taken an adaptive placement test to join your class or practised your grammar with the help of an online learning platform. However, you have probably <u>felt the limitations</u> of relying solely on technology for feedback on your progress, <u>particularly when it comes to the productive skills of speaking and writing</u>. How far can a computer help you with those?

2 If you are studying English – or any other language – in a class with a teacher, the chances are you have been asked to give a presentation to the rest of the class. It is also likely that the presentations you have given have been followed by feedback, first from the other students and then from your teacher. Hopefully, this was a positive experience for you. However, you may have felt that the feedback was either inaccurate or too subjective. Perhaps your classmates did not want you to feel bad, so they said you were amazing or you did not agree with your teacher that you failed to engage your audience. **What if there was a computer programme that could give you a completely objective reaction to your presentation?** How would it work and would you trust it?

3 When we give a presentation – whether in business, in class or for some other purpose – we always hope for a positive reaction from those listening to us. We want our audience to really listen, trust us, engage with us and act on what we have said in some way – maybe to change their way of thinking or to buy our product. Extensive research has helped us understand the ways in which speakers can influence an audience's reaction to them. These include the content of our talk, our body language and how we use our words and voices. Machines can now be trained to measure these factors and give us objective feedback to help us improve our communication skills. One business coach who uses this kind of software to teach presentation skills says: 'Giving feedback with the use of technology is much less personal. You can't argue with a computer!'

4 **Some exam boards have already started to use artificial intelligence to mark students' written work.** Hundreds or even thousands of essays scored by teachers are fed into the computer, which learns to recognise the features of an essay with a particular score. Some studies have shown this to be more accurate than human marking because it eliminates human failings such as tiredness and personal preferences. However, **the whole concept horrifies many working in the classroom.** Teacher and writer Bill Walsh states that, 'At the very least, writing requires a breathing reader.'

5 **The nature of artificial intelligence is that the more data you provide, the better it works.** This means that as time passes and more data is added, the more we will be able to rely on it to give us feedback on our performance. **One of Walsh's objections** to computers marking essays is that they **will not be able to recognise humour, irony, originality of expression or the very subtle differences in meaning between two words.** That may be true at present, but with enough data to work with and the right training, who knows what they might be capable of?

6 **Although performing tasks with the use of artificial intelligence is faster, more cost effective and in many ways more accurate,** there are some limitations **of artificial intelligence which seem impossible to overcome.** Computers are not able to empathise, they do not possess self-awareness and they are poor at multi-tasking. A teacher will be aware that the local football team lost an important match or that students have been delayed in a traffic jam. He or she has access to up-to-the-minute information from a range of sources – and a lifetime of experience in how to react to different situations and different personality types. Artificial intelligence can definitely help teachers but I think they can rest assured that their jobs are safe for a few more years.

2 **Which attitude is expressed by the writer?**

A Professional trainers find computers useful in supporting their feedback to learners.

B Computers are likely to replace teachers in the near future.

3 **Read the article again. Circle the correct words.**

1 Computers are **more useful** when you are practising (**receptive***)/ **productive**** skills.

2 **Feedback from computers** can be more **objective** / **subjective** than feedback from other students.

3 The third paragraph is generally **for** / **against** the use of artificial intelligence in presentation feedback.

4 According to the text, teachers **like** / **dislike** the idea of using artificial intelligence to mark essays.

5 Bill Walsh believes that computers **will** / **will not** be able to recognise sophisticated language.

6 The final paragraph emphasises the **similarities** / **differences** between teachers and computers.

GLOSSARY

*reading and listening
**writing and speaking

HOW WAS THE STARTER UNIT?

Gave it a go	☐
Needed a bit of help	☐
Getting there	☐
Aced it!	☐

1 FIGHTING FIT

GRAMMAR

Scan the QR code and watch the grammar animation.

1 Circle the correct words.

1 I **refuse** joining / (to join) a gym – it's too expensive!

2 Serge **dislikes** playing / to play team games of any type.

3 Olympic athletes **start** training / to train at a very early age.

4 **Stop** playing / to play on the ice. It might break!

5 Have you **managed** losing / to lose any weight yet?

6 Many people **avoid** eating / to eat red meat too often.

2 Match the halves of the sentences. Use different colours.

1	Is this exercise **supposed**	A	**eating** junk food when she was young.
2	Saira **regrets**	B	to hurt this much?
3	The food in Japan **tends**	C	to be healthier than in other countries.

4	**Are** you still **able**	D	eating meals after 8 pm.
5	Everyone should **aim**	E	to eat five portions of fruit or vegetables a day.
6	You should **stop**	F	to touch your toes?

For more help, go to the Grammar reference:
→ **Student's Book** pages 206–207

Scan the QR code and watch the grammar animation.

3 Circle the correct words.

1 Everyone knows that fruit juice contains a lot of sugar. **Although** / (**Nevertheless**) , many people let their children drink it every day.

2 **Instead of** / **While** snacking on biscuits and cake, eat a handful of nuts and seeds. It's much healthier.

3 **Despite** / **Even though** the bad weather, they went ahead with the race.

4 **In spite of** / **Although** he was in pain, Fabio finished the marathon.

5 It can be challenging to follow a healthy diet. **However** / **Whereas**, it is worth it in the long run.

6 You should go for a walk after dinner **despite** / **rather than** sitting on the sofa and watching TV.

4 Read this email to a local government representative.

Complete with the correct words.

whereas   ~~Despite~~   However   Instead of
Although   Unlike in the past

I am a local resident concerned about the health of our children. I don't think the local government is doing enough to protect the younger generation. _Despite_ the fact that the government recommends children eat healthy food, there are eight or nine fast food restaurants in our town! _____, there are still no restaurants which focus on home-cooked, healthy meals at affordable prices. Another problem is the lack of exercise facilities. _____ there are several gyms, they are not open to children under the age of 16. _____ making these facilities adults only, gyms could be encouraged to welcome children at certain times. Our local parks used to be a great place for children to play sports with their friends. _____ , they are not being maintained properly so it is not a good environment for them. There used to be a team of gardeners and maintenance staff, _____ now there is only one person looking after all the parks.

I suggest we make improvements to our town to give our children a healthier future.

1 Match sentences which have the same meaning. Use different colours.

1	It is important **to monitor** how you're doing.	A	It is a good idea to **cut down** on sugar.
2	It can be **very challenging** to lose weight.	B	Right now, I'm totally **out of shape**.
3	You should try to **reduce** the amount of sugar in your diet.	C	Always try to **keep track of** your progress.
4	We **weren't sure** whether our team would win.	D	Losing weight can be **an uphill struggle**.
5	I'm **overweight and unfit** at the moment.	E	It was **touch and go** whether our team would win.

Need help? → **Student's Book** pages 15–17

You are going to read an article about fitness activities. For questions 1 to 10, choose from the activities (A–D). The activities may be chosen more than once.

UNUSUAL FITNESS ACTIVITIES

A Hot yoga

Yoga has long been considered one of the best exercises around, and one that can be practised virtually anywhere, including at home. Hot yoga, as the name suggests, takes it a stage further by turning up the heat, requiring a temperature of around 40°C and humidity of 60%. Clearly, such a change is going to make you sweat more, and this is the whole point as it is supposed to eliminate harmful chemicals and toxins from your body. In a nutshell, hot yoga retains the mental focus of the more traditional version of the discipline but is designed to push your body much harder. The heat increases your heart rate and helps thin the blood, stimulate your metabolism and burn calories at a faster rate. As well as increased strength, stamina and flexibility, practitioners point to a number of other health benefits, such as curing back pain and improving the skin, with many even claiming it has boosted their performance in other sports.

B Aerial fitness

If you ever went to the circus as a child, you probably <u>marvelled at</u> the power and fitness of aerial performers. So if you have ever thought of having a go at such activities yourself, aerial fitness, which is based on similar techniques, may be just what you are looking for. Learners usually start off with the silks, two lengths of fabric attached to the ceiling. Once you have mastered some climbs, you then practise various ways of manoeuvring the body around them, including learning to hang upside down – not something you do every day! More expert practitioners can later progress on to more complex devices, such as hoops, trapezes and slings, and there is even an aerial form of yoga that you can try. Aerial fitness techniques do require you to support your own body weight so clearly the benefits include improved general strength and also increased shoulder mobility. Furthermore, think of the respect you will get from friends and family when you tell them all about it.

C Underwater cycling

Underwater cycling or aqua-cycling combines the concept of a spinning class with the benefits of exercising in water. For those new to the concept, it does literally mean that exercise bicycles are placed in a swimming pool! While spinning, which often involves standing up and bouncing, can create strain on your knees, cycling under water prevents stress on the joints, because the water provides extra support for the body. Unlike spinning too, it is suitable for people of any age, size or shape, even pregnant women and those recovering from injuries, making it perfect for those who find the idea of group exercise a little intimidating.

D Obstacle races

If these were a favourite from your primary school sports day, you can now recreate the fun on a much grander scale. Obstacle races have become fashionable again and you are guaranteed to have a great time with your friends and family while keeping fit. These are usually large-scale, organised events, which can be in urban or rural settings and can involve all kinds of natural and man-made obstacles. You could be jumping over fires, climbing walls or crossing rivers. You might bounce on trampolines, slide down huge water chutes or crawl through tunnels. One thing you can be sure of is that there will be mud – lots of mud! The race might involve dressing up in silly costumes and will probably end with a giant party. Check the internet for events coming up near you.

Which paragraph

1 __B__ is mentioned as being good for impressing others?

2 ___ is described as a bigger version of a competitive event from childhood?

3 ___ is claimed to help remove damaging substances from your body?

4 ___ uses a change of environment to make it less stressful on the body?

5 ___ sees beginners learn to adopt an uncommon body position?

6 ___ is an intentionally more challenging version of a well-known activity?

7 ___ would be fun for anyone who participates, in the writer's opinion?

8 ___ allows users to move on to different equipment as they improve?

9 ___ is claimed to help athletes do better in other sporting disciplines?

10 ___ is appropriate for those who don't necessarily have good levels of fitness?

For more help with Reading and Use of English Part 7: → **Student's Book Exam Focus** page 22

Look at the photos showing young people doing physical activity.

1 Read the student comments.

Underline the key words.

Which photo A or B does each comment correspond to?

1 <u>B</u> It looks <u>a lot riskier</u> and <u>more exciting</u> than the other picture.

2 ___ They can do whatever they want rather than doing what they're told to do.

3 ___ It looks very controlled – everyone looks the same as everyone else.

4 ___ Even though it looks a little boring, it's probably very good exercise.

5 ___ One key difference is that they're out in the fresh air instead of being stuck inside a gym.

6 ___ It looks as though they are at school or in a club.

7 ___ I'd say the chance of injury is much greater.

Photo A

Photo B

2 (Circle) the correct preposition to describe the pictures.

Photo A	
1	I can see some kind of gym equipment **in** / (**at**) **the back of** the photo.
2	The girls are standing **in** / **on the tips of** their toes.
3	There are some ropes **hanging down** to / **from** the ceiling.
4	**In** / **on the background** of the photo there are some ladders.

Photo B	
5	There are buildings **on** / **in either side of** the picture.
6	Both boys are right **in** / **at the middle** of the picture.
7	I can see blue sky **on** / **in the background**.
8	**On** / **In the foreground** there is a rail.

For more help with Speaking Part 2:
→ **Student's Book Speaking bank** page 246

Match the words in bold (1–6) with a similar meaning (A–F). Use different colours.

1	I am interested in taking a course in **nutrition** as I think we all need to watch what we eat.	**A**	**Health** and **happiness**
2	If you are going to run a marathon, you need to improve your **stamina**.	**B**	**Food** and the effect it has on **health**
3	It is important to eat plenty of fruit and vegetables to help your **digestion**.	**C**	The **process** in which the body **breaks down food**
4	If you have bad **posture**, you can suffer from back problems.	**D**	The **ability** to keep going for a long time
5	I think it is important to find a form of exercise that combines both physical and mental **well-being**.	**E**	The **way** someone **sits**, **stands** or **holds themselves**

HOW WAS UNIT 1?

Gave it a go ☐

Needed a bit of help ☐

Getting there ☐

Aced it! ☐

GRAMMAR

Scan the QR code and watch the grammar animation.

used to	be used to	get used to
+ **They** used to go to the sports club often, when they lived in London.	+ I worked in a fast food restaurant so **I was used to** see**ing** lots of customers.	+ **She** got used to study**ing** for exams at university.
- **They** didn't use to have much free time when they lived there.	- I started last week so I'm **not used to** work**ing** at the weekends.	- **He** hasn't got used to study**ing** computer science yet.
? Did **they** use to do a lot of sport?	? Are **you** used to work**ing** at the weekends?	? Are **they** getting used to liv**ing** on campus?
We use used to when we refer to things in the past which are no longer true.	Be used to can refer to past, present and future. It means 'be accustomed' or 'be familiar with'.	Get used to also refers to 'be accustomed' or 'be familiar with' but describes the process.

1 Read the questions and underline the key words.

🔘 04 **Listen to the conversation between Katie and Patrick.**

Write ✓ (true) or ✗ (false).

1 Patrick has <u>fully adjusted</u> to <u>working life</u>. ✗

2 Katie is happy with her salary. ___

3 Patrick and Katie were short of money when they were students. ___

4 Katie used to get up early for her university lectures. ___

5 Patrick finds it easier to get up for work than Katie does. ___

6 As students, Patrick and Katie had to dress smartly. ___

→ 🔘 **Go to page 97 to read the audioscript if you need further help.**

2 (Circle) **the correct verb forms.**

1 In the past, people didn't **used** / **(use)** to lock their front doors when they went out.

2 <u>When my parents arrived</u> in Europe from Jamaica, they found it hard to get **use** / **used** to the cold.

3 <u>I'm from</u> a large family. I**'m used to share** / **sharing** a room.

4 Families **used** / **use** to be much larger – having seven or eight children was quite normal.

5 **Were** / **Did** you use to cycle to school?

6 I **do** / **am not used to** walking so much. I <u>usually</u> drive everywhere.

3 Why is the passive used? Circle the correct answer.

Sometimes both may be possible.

1 My parents' house was broken into a couple of years ago.
   - Ⓐ The speaker doesn't know who did the action.
   - Ⓑ It's not important who did the action.

2 Flour is sieved and added to the mixture.
   - A To show that it is a formal situation.
   - B To describe a process.

3 Manchester United were knocked out by Liverpool.
   - A The speaker doesn't know who did the action.
   - B The speaker is mainly focused on Manchester United.

4 Milk used to be delivered to almost every house in England.
   - A Because we already know that milkmen deliver milk.
   - B Because this is no longer true.

5 A Christmas Carol was written by Charles Dickens.
   - A The speaker is focused on A Christmas Carol.
   - B The speaker is focused on Charles Dickens.

6 I would like to inform you that your loan repayments have not been made for the last two months.
   - A It's a formal situation.
   - B The speaker wants to be indirect.

4 Complete the sentences using the passive form of the verbs.

1	My mum **grew** these tomatoes.	These tomatoes _were grown_ by my mum.
2	Amesh **cooked** this delicious curry.	This delicious curry _____ by Amesh.
3	I think all the students **will understand** the lesson.	I think the lesson _____ by all the students.

4	The teacher **has told me off** three times now.	I _____ by the teacher three times now.
5	Where **did** they **discover** those ruins?	Where _____ those ruins _____?
6	They **are going to make** a new version of the film Titanic.	A new version of the film Titanic _____.

For more help, go to the Grammar reference:
➜ **Student's Book** pages 208–209

VOCABULARY

1 Complete the sentences with the correct words.

~~nephew~~ stepdaughter granddaughter
siblings sister-in-law father-in-law

1 My brother has a son. He is my
nephew .

2 Tim married Rosie, who already
had a daughter called Chloe from
a previous marriage. Chloe is Tim's
_____ .

3 Ana is married to Claudio. Claudio's
father is Santiago. Santiago is Ana's
_____ .

4 My husband has a sister called Julia.
Julia is my _____ .

5 I've got two _____ , one
brother and one sister.

6 Alberto's daughter has a girl
called Sofia. Sofia is Alberto's
_____ .

Need help? ➔ **Student's Book** page 31

2 Match the questions to the answers. Use different colours.

1	Have you ever **fallen out** with a friend?	A	Yes, we often **go out** for a coffee together after the lesson.
2	Do you **get on well** with the other students in your class?	B	My dad, definitely. **We're both** tall with dark, curly hair.
3	Who do you **take after** in your family?	C	Yes, I once **stopped talking** to Derek for a month!

4	Who do you **look up to** in your family?	D	I usually **hang out** with my friends.
5	What do you **get up to** at weekends?	E	No, I'm not sure that would be a **good idea**.
6	Have you ever met up with someone you **met online**?	F	My older sister. She's a **really brilliant** student.

Need help? ➔ **Student's Book** page 34

LISTENING PART 4

STRATEGY

- Read the questions before you listen.
- Highlight or underline the key words in each question.
- Draw lines to separate A, B and C.

🔊 05 **You will hear an interview with psychologist Antonia Russo, who is talking about the influence of birth order on personality. For questions 1–7, choose the best answer (A, B or C).**

1 What led Dr Russo to become interested in birth order and personality?

   A her own two children

   (B) her childhood experiences

   C her role as a psychologist

2 One possible reason for the success of firstborn children is that

   A they get more attention from their parents.

   B they are naturally more gifted.

   C they tend to be more interested in creative activities.

3 According to Dr Russo, the youngest child may

   A have problems with their identity.

   B be lacking in self-confidence.

   C be good at getting their own way.

4 How did being the middle child affect Dr Russo?

   A She became very close to her sisters.

   B She didn't get noticed by her family.

   C She sometimes went against her parents.

5 What does Dr Russo say about only children?

   A They are generally the most spoilt.

   B They share similar characteristics to firstborns.

   C They are usually the best leaders.

6 What does Dr Russo think about the role that gender plays in influencing children's personalities?

   A She feels that not enough research has been done in this area.

   B She believes that parents need to consider this when raising their children.

   C She doubts whether it affects the way that children develop.

7 Dr Russo sums up by saying that

   A birth order strongly influences personality.

   B the development of personality is complex.

   C further studies on birth order are needed.

→ 🔊 Go to page 97 to read the audioscript if you need further help.

For more help with Listening Part 4:
→ **Student's Book Exam Focus** page 37

WRITING PART 1

1 Look at the Writing Part 1 question.

In your English class you have watched a documentary about families with lots of children. Your teacher has asked you to write an essay giving your opinion on large families.

What are the advantages and disadvantages of being a member of a large family?

Notes

Write about:

		advantages	disadvantages
1	having a ready-made social network		
2	the problem of lacking space and privacy		
3	… (your own idea)		

Which opening paragraph is the most suitable, A or B?

A If you are part of a large family, you will have a ready-made social network. You are sure to get on well with at least some of your siblings. The problem would be if you didn't have a big enough house because you wouldn't get enough space to keep your things. You might be interrupted by your little brothers and sisters when you were trying to do your homework.

B In the past, it was common for families to have many children. Nowadays, though, the average in developed countries is between one and two children per family. However, there are some couples who choose not to follow this trend and have large numbers of children. What would it be like to be a child with many siblings?

2 Read the rest of the essay.

Complete the gaps with the correct words or phrases.

For me	it doesn't matter whether
Finally	One of the main drawbacks
~~There is no doubt that~~	

<u>There is no doubt that</u> **children with many siblings are never lonely**. They do not need to arrange to meet up with friends or join clubs because there is a ready-made social circle at home. Furthermore, small children will be cared for by older brothers and sisters as well as by their parents.

_____ of life in a big family would be the lack of space and privacy. It might be difficult to find a quiet spot to do your homework and it would not really be possible to invite friends round to such a crowded home. _____, sharing a room with one or more siblings would be the worst part and I believe this would cancel out the positive aspects.

_____, growing up in a large family develops positive characteristics. Children will not be spoilt by being given everything they want. They have to share and help others from an early age.

In my opinion, _____ your family is big or small. What matters is to have a happy family.

THINK BACK

☐ How many paragraphs are there?

☐ Does it talk about having a ready-made social network?

☐ Does the essay talk about lack of space and privacy?

☐ Does it present advantages and disadvantages?

For more help with Writing Part 1:
➔ **Student's Book Writing bank** page 234

For more help with Writing Part 1:
➔ **Student's Book Writing bank** page 234

Match sentences which have the same meaning. Use different colours.

1	People **have said** that **social media** has had a negative impact on our lives.	A	It **could be argued** that **friendship** is **less sincere** nowadays.
2	People **have suggested** that **online friends** aren't real friends.	B	It **is believed** that **social media** will become **less popular** in the future.
3	People **argue** that **friendship** is **less sincere** nowadays.	C	It **has been said** that **social media** has had a negative impact on our lives.
4	People **have said** that **families** are **growing** further **apart**.	D	It **has been suggested** that **online friends** aren't real friends.
5	People **believe** that **social media** will become **less popular** in the future.	E	It **has been said** that **families** are **growing** further **apart**.

HOW WAS UNIT 2?

Gave it a go	☐
Needed a bit of help	☐
Getting there	☐
Aced it!	☐

3 BEYOND THE CLASSROOM

GRAMMAR

Scan the QR code and watch the grammar animation.

1 🎧 06 **Listen to a teacher giving advice to a student, who is planning to study medicine.**

Tick (✓) the advice she gives.

1 Find out how doctors work. ✓

2 Use online resources to get information.

3 You only need to do one work experience placement.

4 Make contact with students in a similar situation to yours.

5 Concentrate only on your studies.

6 Start visiting universities you'd like to apply to.

→ 🎧 Go to page 99 to read the audioscript if you need further help.

First conditional: to express a future situation which we think is real or possible.

If + present simple and will/can + infinitive

If I apply now, I will get an interview.

Second conditional: to talk about things which are imaginary, contrary to the facts, impossible or improbable.

If + past simple and would/could + infinitive

If I saved more money, I could buy a new car.

---

2 **Complete the sentences with the first or second conditional. Use the verbs in the box.**

learn	join	need	~~pass~~	quit	not work

1 If I ___pass___ my exam, I will be happy.

2 I would _____ a gym if I didn't have classes all the time.

3 If you _____ hard, you won't be able to get the grades you want.

4 I _____ to play the guitar if I had the time.

5 You'll _____ to get a visa if you want to study in China.

6 I _____ my job if I could afford to.

3 **Complete the sentences with the correct form of the verbs.**

1 Provided he achieves his predicted grades, William (start) _will start_ college in September.

2 As soon as I (finish) _____ my homework, I'm going out.

3 The run will take place on Sunday, assuming it (not rain) _____ .

4 What if someone (offer) _____ to do your assignment for you? Would you accept?

5 You (be able to) _____ enrol on that course unless you have passed your exams.

For more help, go to the Grammar reference:
→ **Student's Book** pages 210-211

VOCABULARY

1 **Complete the word families table.**

~~experience~~ graduate tutor study educate experiment

Noun(s)	Verb(s)	Adjective(s)
experience	_experience_	experiential
_____	experiment	experimental
education, educator	_____	educational, educated
study, student	_____	studious
_____, graduation	graduate	graduate
tutor, tutorial	_____	tutorial

2 **Complete the sentences with the correct words.**

~~experiments~~ experience studious graduation educate tutorials

1 Being a **scientist** means you often need to conduct _experiments_ .

2 I attended my sister's _____ **ceremony** yesterday. We were all so proud of her.

3 At university, you have **different classes** called lectures, seminars and _____ .

4 She has a lot of _____ in medicine. She's been a doctor **for 30 years**.

5 Amina is a very _____ girl. She is **always reading books** and **never forgets her homework**.

6 It is important to _____ children about the **importance of** protecting the environment.

3 **Match the sentences (1–7) with the idioms (A–G) that describe them.**

1	I got 100% on my recent English exam.	A	I **went the extra mile**.
2	I stayed up all night in order to finish the project.	B	I am a **bookworm**.
3	I love reading books about biology.	C	I **passed with flying colours**.
4	I worked for 10 hours more than I should have.	D	I **pulled an all-nighter**.

5	I memorised all the tenses in English.	E	I am **over the moon**.
6	I'm so happy about my exam result.	F	I am the **teacher's pet**.
7	I am my teacher's favourite student.	G	I **learnt** them **by heart**.

Need help? → Student's Book page 47

4 Complete the sentences with the correct words.

a̶ ̶s̶t̶u̶d̶y̶   campus   lecture theatre
dissertation   graduation ceremony
resit

1   The university recently **published**
    ___a study___ which looks at the
    effects exams have on young learners.

2   Unfortunately, my sister has **failed**
    one of her **exams** so she needs to
    _____ it next month.

3   There's plenty of **accommodation** for
    students on _____ , which means
    that we **won't have far to go** to get to
    our lectures every morning.

4   I submitted my _____ yesterday.
    It was a total of 15,000 words, which is
    by far the longest **piece of writing** I've
    ever had to do.

5   The _____ will
    take place in the Hawking Building.
    Students are allowed to bring up to
    four **guests**.

6   The **presentation** will be held in the
    main _____ and will
    last for approximately **one hour**.

Need help? → **Student's Book** page 45

Read the conditional sentences.

Choose the correct answer.

Write the letter.

1   _B_ sell you the answers to the
    exam, please let your teacher know
    immediately.
    A   Was anyone try to
    B   Should anyone try to

2   ___ by the university of your choice,
    I am sure you will be able to find
    another excellent one to go to.
    A   Should you not be accepted
    B   Shouldn't you accepted

3   I would be very angry ___ that
    your homework was copied from
    another student.
    A   were I finding out
    B   were I to find out

4   ___ a student identity card, you
    won't be able to register with the
    library.
    A   Should you not have
    B   Weren't you have

5   ___ a question during the exam,
    please raise your hand and wait for
    the examiner to come to your desk.
    A   Were you have
    B   Should you have

SPEAKING PART 3

1 🎧 07 **Listen to two students, Mario and Yuriko, doing the first part of the Part 3 task below. For each factor shown, decide if they agree (A) or disagree (D) on how important it is.**

Job opportunities
___D___

Facilities
_____

Why might these factors be important to students when choosing a college or university?

Reputation
_____

Location
_____

Cost
_____

2 **Look at the expressions in the table. Choose the correct headings.**

Partial agreement / disagreement
Showing disagreement   Giving clarification
~~Showing agreement~~

Showing agreement	_____
I'd go along with that. I see your point.	I'm afraid I completely disagree with you there. I'm not so sure about that.
_____	_____
I suppose you might be right. I agree up to a point.	It means … What I mean by that is …

3 🎧 08 **Now listen to the second part of the Part 3 task. Write ✓ (true) or ✗ (false).**

1 Mario thinks it is **easy** to decide which **factor** to **choose**.   ✗

2 Mario and Yuriko agree that **location** and **cost** are **less important** factors.   _____

3 Mario believes that the **principal motivation** for university students is **finding employment**.   _____

4 Yuriko **does not think** students really **care** much about **reputation** or **facilities**.   _____

5 In the end, they **agree** together on **one factor** as the **most important**.   _____

6 Yuriko **believes** that **employers** take the **reputation** of universities **into account**.   _____

→ Go to pages 99–100 to read the audioscripts if you need further help.

> **❗ EXAM TIP**
>
> Remember that in Part 3 what matters is the discussion, not whether you agree with your partner. Make sure that you express and justify opinions but also that you take turns to speak and respond to what each other says, including agreeing / disagreeing and asking for clarification.

For more help with Speaking Part 3:
→ **Student's Book Speaking bank** page 250

READING AND USE OF ENGLISH PART 6

> ⓘ **STRATEGY**
>
> - Read the question carefully.
> - Focus on the paragraphs with the gaps. Cover the others if you need to.
> - Look at the sentences before and after the gap.
> - Highlight or <u>underline</u> any key vocabulary.
> - Choose the missing sentence.
> - When you finish draw lines through the sentence so you don't use it again.
> - Remember there is one sentence you do not need.

You are going to read a magazine article about an innovative school in New York.

Six sentences have been removed from it.

Choose from the sentences A to G the one that fits each gap (1–6).

There is one extra sentence you do not need to use.

Schools of the future

Educational psychologist Neil Akidil visits a school with a modern approach to teaching and learning.

Although society has changed dramatically with the advent of information technology, education has not changed as much as might have been expected.

Classrooms now contain computers, but there is more that is the same about education now compared with 60 years ago than is different.

(1) ___E___ A typical school day is divided into periods for different subjects, which are studied in isolation. There may be occasional projects, but these are often pushed to the sidelines and not allowed to get in the way of the 'real' work of completing the academic syllabus.

The Portfolio School in Tribeca, New York is different and may give us a glimpse into the schools of the future.

(2) _____ This method is centred around an interdisciplinary model of learning, and project work is central to the approach. Children are not divided into grades by age and the school day is not divided into subjects.

Instead, the year is broken into 'learning units' lasting three or four months, each of which can be approached from a variety of angles. (3) _____ So, for example, in a lesson on colour, the students designed and made a lightbox projector and programmed an LED bonfire.

The Portfolio School has other differences from regular schools, too. There is no homework – research has shown it is not very useful. Teachers are not seen as the possessors of knowledge which they then pass on to their students. **(4)** _____ According to the school, their approach causes deep learning to occur in children, fuelled by genuine curiosity rather than obligation. The philosophy of the school is based on preparing children for the actual world they will live in, which is technological, global and entrepreneurial. There is an emphasis on thinking skills and self-reflection, which are vital in the modern world.

The parents of children who attend the school are delighted with their children's progress. The system focuses on creating a need for learning, rather than teachers simply teaching facts from a pre-defined syllabus. **(5)** _____ However, at Portfolio, this soon changed. When the same child wanted to build a model, she quickly realised that in order to do so she needed to learn how to carry out certain measurements and calculations. Suddenly she had a motivation to learn maths and now, a few months on, she loves the subject. Her father points to his daughter's developing educational independence and says that these days she 'skips to school'.

The Portfolio School is sadly, not accessible to everyone. (6) _____ However, the school is keen to reach out to the wider community and serve as a model of what education can be. The school may have world-class facilities, including 3D printers for the children to use, but they emphasise that these are just tools. It is the philosophy and approach that makes the school what it is. In theory, this could be replicated anywhere. So, the question is, will all schools look like Portfolio in the future?

A	For example, one mother highlighted the fact that her daughter had struggled at maths at regular schools because of the lack of practical application of the subject.
B	The annual fees of $35,000 are discouraging for the vast majority of parents and the student capacity of the school is limited.
C	There are tests but children can take them any time they feel ready and they mark them themselves.
D	The school's approach is research-based and has been developed by an impressive panel of experts in learning and child development.
E	Students still generally sit in rows with a teacher at the front and the curriculum is specified in advance, usually by governments or local authorities.
F	Rather, they are considered mentors who guide and assist the learners.
G	The focus is always on creativity, design and practical learning.

For more help with Reading and Use of English Part 6: → **Student's Book Exam Focus** page 36

HOW WAS UNIT 3?

Gave it a go ☐

Needed a bit of help ☐

Getting there ☐

Aced it! ☐

4 A TRIP TO REMEMBER

VOCABULARY

1 Complete the sentences with the correct words.

~~commuters~~   jet lag   departure lounge
cockpit   motorists   diesel   motorway

1   The **train** was **cancelled**, which annoyed a lot of the _commuters_ who were **waiting** for it.

2   I've just come back from a **trip** to New York and now I'm **suffering from** _____ .

3   The **plane** was delayed on the runway so the **pilots let us sit** in the _____ .

4   **Cars** that run on _____ are considered to be more harmful to the environment than those that run on **petrol**.

5   Although I've passed my **driving test**, I still get really nervous about **driving on the** _____ .

6   I was **sitting** in the _____ when they **announced** that our flight had been cancelled.

7   They **introduced** a **car sharing** scheme in the city **to reduce** the number of _____ on the roads.

2 Match words and make collocations. Use different colours.

1	prepare for	A	a gap
2	run on	B	landing
3	overtake	C	diesel
4	leave	D	the car in front

5	hold	E	the handlebars
6	avoid	F	the environment
7	harm	G	on the runway
8	taxi	H	the rush hour traffic

Need help? → Student's Book pages 56–57

3 Circle the correct words.

1   We booked our hotel at the (last) / **long** minute so we got a really good deal.

2   The room wasn't **air** / **part** conditioned so we had difficulty sleeping at night due to the heat.

3   I work **cut** / **part** time as a shop assistant during the school holidays.

4   Despite the jet lag, I quite enjoy **far** / **long** distance air travel.

5   The company went bankrupt so they were offering **cut** / **last** price deals on all their package holidays.

6   The visitor **attraction** / **recreation** proved to be a big success with tourists.

Need help? → Student's Book page 62

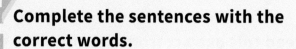

Complete the sentences with the correct words.

Life   lives

1   They say that cats have nine _lives_ .
    Life is what you make it.

gear   gears

2   Did you remember to bring your sports
    _____?
    How many _____ does your bike
    have?

times   time

3   I haven't got _____ to finish my
    homework.
    I've been to Italy three _____ .

business   businesses

4   Small _____ are finding it hard to
    survive.
    Sam studied _____ at university.

room   rooms

5   Do you think there'll be _____
    there for all my books?
    We lived in a small flat when I was
    young – there were only three
    _____ .

GRAMMAR

Scan the QR codes and watch the grammar animations.

1 **Read this extract from a tour guide. Write a, an, the or – (no article) in each gap.**

The Maldives is one of **(1)** _____ most unique countries in the world. It is made up of 1,192 islands, spread over 90,000 square kilometres. The capital, Malé, is unusual in that it is not **(2)** _____ tourist destination. It is less than six square miles, yet it is home to over **(3)** _____ third of the country's population of about 430,000. Only 185 of the islands are inhabited by local people. Tourism accounts for **(4)** _____ most of the country's economy. The sun-drenched islands and coral reefs teeming with tropical fish attract tourists all year round. The Maldives is particularly popular with couples looking for **(5)** _____ amazing place to get married. The Maldives is not **(6)** _____ budget destination, however. It has some of the most expensive and luxurious hotels in the world.

2 **Put each noun into the correct column in the table.**

~~things~~ ~~rice~~ ~~pain~~ data cash virus life crash business room pedal footprint stuff resort scenery voyage land time chaos gear

Countable	Uncountable	Both
things	rice	pain

For more help, go to the Grammar reference:
→ **Student's Book** pages 212–213

🎧 09 **You will hear people talking in eight different situations. For questions 1–8, choose the best answer (A, B or C).**

1. You hear a man talking about a journey. How did he travel?
   - A   by bus
   - B   by plane
   - C   by train

2. You hear two people talking about the local bus service. What do they say about it?
   - A   The fares are too expensive.
   - B   The seats are uncomfortable.
   - C   The drivers are rude.

3. You hear two people talking about a place they have just visited. What kind of place is it?
   - A   an art gallery
   - B   a cinema
   - C   a shop

4. You hear a travel agent talking to a man about a holiday. What does she advise him to do?
   - A   purchase travel insurance
   - B   book excursions in advance
   - C   take warm clothing

5. You hear a man talking to a friend about a travel programme he has recently watched. What does he say about the programme?
   - A   It gave lots of useful advice.
   - B   It was better than he had expected.
   - C   It made him decide to visit a place.

6. You hear a woman talking about somewhere she has visited. What point is she making?
   - A   It appeals more to children than adults.
   - B   It reminded her of her childhood.
   - C   It is similar to another place she has visited.

7. You hear a man phoning a hotel. What does he want to find out?
   - A   how good the local services are
   - B   whether the hotel is suitable for children
   - C   when the restaurant opens in the evening

8. You hear a woman talking about a cruise she went on. What didn't she like about it?
   - A   the lack of variety
   - B   the food on board
   - C   the places they visited

➜ 🎧 Go to page 101 to read the audioscript if you need further help.

For more help with Listening Part 1:
➜ **Student's Book Exam Focus** page 52

1 🔊 10 **Listen to four speakers answer a question.**

Match the speakers to the question they answer.

A   What do you do in the school holidays? _3_

B   Can you tell me about the place you come from? ___

C   What type of holiday would you like to go on? ___

D   How do you usually go to school? ___

2 ▶ 10 Listen again to the speakers. Complete the sentences.

Speaker 1

1 It's a _sleepy_ little place, with just one shop, a school and not much else really.

2 There's no water close by, no lakes or rivers, so many people have swimming pools in their gardens because it's absolutely _boiling_ in summer.

Speaker 2

3 I haven't passed my driving test yet so I usually take the bus or **t**_____ to school.

4 In the summer I might walk if I've got the **e**_____ , but that's not very often!

Speaker 3

5 It depends on the **s**_____ .

6 During the winter holidays, we just **h**_____ out at each other's houses or go out for pizza or something like that.

Speaker 4

7 I'd probably **c**_____ a city break as I live in the countryside and big cities are much more exciting.

8 I'd definitely want to stay right in the centre, where all the **a**_____ is.

➔ ▶ Go to page 102 to read the audioscript if you need further help.

3 Read the sentences. Which advice is good? Circle your opinion.

1 Don't speak too quickly or too slowly. Slow down for important points and speed up a bit for less important details. 👍 👎

2 Stay up all night watching English films the night before the test. 👍 👎

3 Part 1 is just a practice so don't bother giving full answers. 👍 👎

4 You must speak only to the other candidate in Part 1. 👍 👎

5 Try to use a variety of vocabulary and grammar. 👍 👎

6 In Part 1 you might be asked Yes/No questions. You will still need to explain your answers and give examples and explanations. 👍 👎

For more help with Speaking Part 1:
➔ **Student's Book Speaking Bank** page 244

HOW WAS UNIT 4?

Gave it a go	☐
Needed a bit of help	☐
Getting there	☐
Aced it!	☐

5 GRAB SOME CULTURE

GRAMMAR

Scan the QR code and watch the grammar animation.

1 **Complete the sentences with the correct form of the** past simple**,** past perfect simple **or** past perfect continuous**.**

1 I **(begin)** _began_ learning English at school in 2014, but I'd already learnt many words by listening to songs in the language.

2 They suddenly realised that they **(forgot)** _____ their homework.

3 Mia **(play)** _____ only _____ the violin for two years when she was invited to join her local orchestra.

4 The teacher asked me whether I **(complete)** _____ the exercise.

5 When I **(see)** _____ the film at the cinema, it had been available online for a few weeks.

6 I **(think)** _____ about quitting my job before my friend told me that it wasn't a good idea.

7 They **(already / eat)** _____ their dinner by the time their father got home.

2 Circle **the correct verbs.**

1 I **was** / **had been** tired last night because I had been studying in the library the whole day.

2 We **ate already** / **had already eaten** a big steak so I didn't really fancy eating dessert.

3 We had been **look** / **looking** for our cat, Joe, for three hours before we found him asleep under the bed.

4 We were disappointed to hear that the show had been **cancelled** / **cancelling**.

5 She asked if she could borrow my tablet but I had already **lend** / **lent** it to someone else.

6 I had just finished my assignment when I realised that I **written** / **had written** about the wrong topic.

For more help, go to the Grammar reference:
→ **Student's Book** page 214

VOCABULARY

1 **Tick (✓) two phrases that match each description.**

1	I haven't been out all weekend because I downloaded Yellow Crocus by Laila Ibrahim. I wasn't able to do anything else until I'd finished it. She's written other novels but I absolutely loved this book – I'll definitely read anything else she writes.	I couldn't put it down ✓ a real page-turner ✓ confusing
2	I know they are for children but I still find Roald Dahl's books really clever and they always make me laugh uncontrollably. More than 250 million copies of his books have been sold. I still have all my old copies and I sometimes pick them up and read a bit before I sleep. They help me relax.	best-selling author bedtime reading she got me hooked
3	We had to read it for school but I didn't enjoy it at all. There was too much detailed description of every little thing. Our teacher explained how much skill the writer had used and how much care had gone into every detail of the structure, but I couldn't really get what the author was trying to say half the time.	have me in stitches tedious heavy-going

Need help? ➜ **Student's Book** pages 70-71

2 **Complete the conversation between Nina and Charlie.**

Use the correct words.

> gripping   deals with   vital   awful   ~~set in~~   dull

Nina: Have you been watching that new drama series? The one ___set in___ Sweden.

Charlie: You mean the one where that family gets lost in the mountains? I watched one episode but I thought it was _____, to be honest. It was so unbelievable and no-one in it could act.

Nina: You're kidding! It _____ _____ some really important issues.

Charlie: Important issues? Such as what?

Nina: Well, if you had seen the second episode, you would have learnt a lot about how climate change has affected the environment in northern Europe.

Charlie: How very _____ ! When you said important issues, I thought you meant social issues, not boring things like that.

Nina: How can you say that? Looking after the environment is _____ . Despite what you say, I think it's great. It's really _____ . I haven't missed a single episode.

Need help? ➜ **Student's Book** page 74

Read the sentences 1–6.

Focus on the word in bold.

Match the words in bold (1–6)
with a similar meaning (A–F).
Use different colours.

1	I found the book Never Let Me Go really **gripping**. I just couldn't put it down.	A	twists
2	Leonardo Di Caprio is an **exceptional** actor. He plays every role brilliantly.	B	dense
3	I found the story quite difficult to follow. There were too many **complications** for my liking.	C	outstanding
4	Dickens tells some marvellous stories but some of his books are very **heavy-going**.	D	absorbing

5	In my view, that book is **compulsory reading** for everyone.	E	minor role
6	I had a **small part** in my school play.	F	contemporary
7	I prefer **modern** literature to the classics.	G	a must-read

> **❗ STRATEGY**
> - Read the text.
> - Look at options A, B, C and D.
> - Look at the gap. Decide which type of word fits.
> - Then look at the options.
> - When you decide which letter to use, write it next to the number.

For questions 1–8, read the text below and decide which answer (A, B, C or D) best fits each gap. There is an example at the beginning (0).

Art installations

An installation is more an experience than a **(0)** _B_ of art. **(1)**___ a painting or sculpture is created in the artist's studio and transported to a gallery, an installation is designed to fit a particular space. Many installations take up an entire room in a gallery, but they could also be **(2)**___ in the open. Installations put the viewer at the centre of the artwork. You may be able to walk through the space and the artist may **(3)**___ to different senses. There may be **(4)**___ of performance art, such as dance or mime, and nowadays computer technology may play a part. Recycled materials are often used, as **(5)**___ natural elements.

Many installations are designed to **(6)**___ a concept rather than simply to be beautiful. Many **(7)**___ of this kind have been produced to support charities. Modern spectators engage with installations because they are now used to **(8)**___ in these kinds of experiences.

0	**A** section	**(B)** piece	**C** part			**D** element
1	**A** However	**B** Whereas	**C** When			**D** Unless
2	**A** taken up	**B** got up	**C** set up			**D** looked up
3	**A** appeal	**B** use	**C** design			**D** attract
4	**A** views	**B** issues	**C** roles			**D** aspects
5	**A** is	**B** are	**C** do			**D** have
6	**A** speak	**B** commit	**C** communicate			**D** persuade
7	**A** works	**B** arts	**C** performances			**D** actions
8	**A** enjoying	**B** viewing	**C** involving			**D** participating

For more help with Reading and Use of English Part 1:
→ **Student's Book Exam Focus** page 64

1 **Read the Writing Part 2 task and a student's answer to the question.**

   Tick (✓) the questions the student answers.

You see this notice on an English-language website.

Articles wanted!

Your favourite art form

What is your favourite art form? ✓

How did you become interested in it?

What do you like about it?

Who would you recommend it to?

We will publish the best articles on our website!

Write your article.

---

1   One of my favourite art forms is ballet. I first (got into) it when I was about 8 years old and my parents took me to watch a performance at the local theatre. It was outstanding! From then on, I was hooked. I begged my mum to let me go to ballet classes after school and I was thrilled when she did.

2   Ballet is elegant and graceful. The dancers seem quite fragile, but don't be fooled. Ballerinas are top-class athletes, who train for many years to become the best at what they do. One of the reasons I love ballet so much is how effortless they make it look.

3   If you're a fan of a good story and classical music, then ballet is for you. That being said, I would encourage everyone to go and see a ballet show at some point in their lives.

2 Answer the questions

Which paragraph:

A gives information about ballet dancers? ___

B describes how the student started ballet? ___

C recommends seeing a ballet? ___

3 (Circle) the words in the article which mean the following.

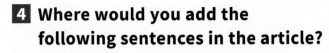

1 became interested (paragraph 1)

2 really good (paragraph 1)

3 addicted (paragraph 1)

4 stylish (paragraph 2)

5 beautiful (paragraph 2)

6 easily done (paragraph 2)

7 someone who admires or supports something (paragraph 3)

8 at some moment in time (paragraph 3)

4 Where would you add the following sentences in the article?

		Paragraph number	After sentence number
1	Here, I learnt a lot about the basics of ballet.	1	5
2	They also follow a strict diet to stay in the best possible shape.		
3	This is even more impressive when you consider that it's one of the most physically demanding art forms in the world.		
4	Trust me, you won't be disappointed.		

For more help with Writing Part 2: Article:
→ **Student's Book Writing bank** page 240

HOW WAS UNIT 5?

Gave it a go ☐

Needed a bit of help ☐

Getting there ☐

Aced it! ☐

6 CLOSER TO NATURE

GRAMMAR

Scan the QR code and watch the grammar animation.

1 Match the halves of the sentences. Use different colours.

1	There are millions of **species**	A	**where** we should have the picnic.
2	That beautiful **park** is the place	B	**which** are characterised by high rainfall.
3	Rainforests are **forests**	C	**which** still haven't been discovered.
4	My friend Rebecca is an **equine vet**,	D	**which** means she treats sick horses.

5	I'd like you to meet **Mr Jennings**,	E	**who** my mother takes our dog to.
6	That's the **lion cub**	F	**who** is the gardener here.
7	He's the **dog trainer**	G	**which** the rangers released into the wild.

2 Read the rules. Circle the correct words.

Defining relative clauses:

are clauses which tell us which **(particular)** / **general** person or thing the speaker is talking about.

give **essential** / **extra** information.

do / **don't** have commas.

do / **don't** use the following relative pronouns: who, which, whose, where, when and why.

can / **can't** use 'that' instead of 'who' or 'which'.

Who, which or that **can** / **cannot** be omitted when they are the object of the clause.

Non-defining relative clauses:

give us **extra** / **(specific)** information.

use / **don't use** commas (or pauses in spoken English).

use / **don't use** the following relative pronouns: who, which, whose, where and when.

do / **don't** use that.

The relative pronoun **can** / **cannot** be omitted.

3 Complete the sentences with the correct relative pronouns.

1   I have never been back to the **place** ___where___ I was born.

2   The **safari park**, _____ was one of the first in the country, has closed down.

3   I would love to have **a job** _____ involved working with animals.

4   That's **the scientist** _____ I was telling you about last week.

5   The **building**, _____ they made the scientific discovery, is being demolished.

4 Complete the sentences with the correct phrases.

| on which   for which   both of whom |
| ~~all of which~~   neither of which |
| one of which |

1   There are four species of zebra, __all of which__ are declining in number.

2   I grew up in the countryside, _____ I am very grateful.

3   We have three cats, _____ is a Siamese.

4   I have two sisters, _____ like gardening.

5   Julie has a guide dog, _____ she is totally dependent.

6   We have two pear trees in our garden, _____ bears fruit.

5 Complete the sentences with the correct words.

| of   on   as   ~~from~~   against   of |

1   We need to **prevent** the black rhino ___from___ dying out.

2   I don't **approve** _____ testing cosmetic products on animals.

3   The farmer **warned** us _____ entering the field with the bull.

4   The city is **regarded** _____ one of the most beautiful places to live in the world.

5   Bees are **capable** _____ producing only small amounts of honey.

6   My father **insists** _____ cutting the grass every weekend.

For more help, go to the Grammar reference:
→ **Student's Book** pages 216–217

Circle one or both of the complex prepositions.

1   Photographers stayed up all night **(in the hope of)** / **by means of** getting pictures of the new-born lion cubs.

2   I love all animals **(apart from)** / **(except for)** snakes.

3   The pregnant panda is being moved to a new enclosure **ahead of** / **in front of** the birth.

4   I am writing **with regard to** / **in relation to** my recent visit to your wildlife park.

5   We made our decision **on the basis of** / **on account of** your previous experience with animals.

6   Richard went on the school trip to the zoo **on account of** / **along with** all the other students in his class.

VOCABULARY

1 **Match each heading to the correct group of words (1–6).**

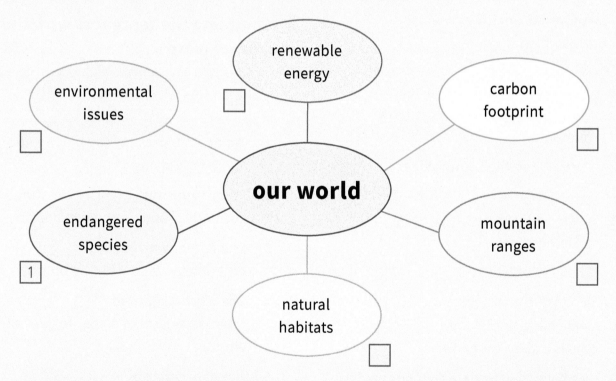

1   ~~tiger, polar bear, mountain gorilla, bluefin tuna~~

2   forest, desert, grassland, wetland

3   the Himalayas, the Alps, the Andes

4   climate change, water pollution, overfishing

5   solar, wind, hydropower, bioenergy

6   travel by plane, use a computer, use plastic bags

Need help? → **Student's Book** page 83

2 Circle the correct words.

1. We've just come back from a wonderful **travel** / **trip** to the Caribbean.

2. Please **say** / **tell** me what you think about the video I've just posted.

3. The closure of the zoo will have a negative **choice** / **effect** on the local economy.

4. The locals gave us some really good **choice** / **advice** on the best places to visit.

5. I persuaded my cousin to let me **borrow** / **lend** her camera for my trip.

6. A lot of people often **advice** / **choose** to stay in hostels because they're cheaper than hotels.

Need help? → **Student's Book** page 88

3 Complete the blog post with the correct words.

border ~~capital~~ famous habitat heading range memorable ~~unforgettable~~ vehicles wildlife

Last month, my family and I went on a safari holiday to Africa. It was such an ___unforgettable___ experience. We flew into Nairobi, which is the ____capital____ of Kenya, and then took a bus to Lake Nakuru. I had seen flamingos in the zoo close to where I live but it was so much better seeing them in their natural _____ . There were hundreds of them! We spent a few days there before _____ south, through Nairobi, to Amboseli National Park. It's a stunning place, located on the Kenya-Tanzania _____ . It's also close to Mount Kilimanjaro, which is the highest peak in the world that is not part of a mountain _____ , standing at a height of 5,895 metres above sea level. The park is _____ for being one of the best places in the world to see elephants and we spent five days there, travelling through the park. We weren't allowed to leave our _____ at any point, which was understandable as there are very strict rules in place to protect the _____ there. Sadly, after ten _____ days in Kenya, we had to fly back home. I hope I can go back there again one day as it's one of the most beautiful places in the world.

! STRATEGY

- Read the statements and underline the key words.
- Remember there are three statements you do not need.
- Cross out the statements when you match them.
- Remember you can listen twice.

11 **You will hear five people talking about their experience of being a volunteer. For questions 1–5, choose from the list (A–H) how each speaker feels about their experience. Use the letters only once. There are three extra letters which you do not need to use.**

A proud of what they achieved

B embarrassed by a mistake they made

C annoyed by a person they worked with

D irritated by the lack of organisation

E impressed with the training they received

F bored by having to do the same thing many times

G relieved that they managed to complete the programme

H ~~inspired by the feedback they got~~

Speaker 1 _H_

Speaker 2 ___

Speaker 3 ___

Speaker 4 ___

Speaker 5 ___

For more help with Listening part 3:
→ **Student's Book Exam Focus** page 77

→ Go to page 103 to read the audioscript if you need further help.

WRITING PART 2: REVIEW

1 **A student called Monty has written a review of a TV programme he watched. Complete the review with the correct adjectives.**

> challenging   deadly   hilarious
> ~~entertaining~~   shaky   serious

Recently, I watched a documentary called Urban Monkeys. It was about monkeys who live in the cities of India. It was extremely **(1)** _entertaining_ as the animals tried every trick they could think of to get hold of food. **The best bit** was when a whole load of monkeys got into a school and somehow managed to open the children's lunch boxes and eat everything. It was **(2)** _____ .

Although the programme was very amusing, there was a **(3)** _____ side to it as well. These creatures are a nuisance in Indian cities and can damage people's livelihoods. **In addition**, they carry **(4)** _____ diseases so they pose a real threat to the inhabitants of these cities.

It must have been **(5)** _____ to film this documentary because the monkeys move around very quickly and they can climb onto buildings. At times, the camerawork was a bit **(6)** _____ but you can't really blame the cameraman for that.

Overall, it was a fascinating programme for all the family.

2 **Look at the bold words in Monty's text.**

Which words does he use to do these things?

1 say when he watched this programme — _recently_

2 introduce his favourite part — _____

3 introduce an opposite idea — _____

4 introduce a similar point — _____

5 introduce his conclusion — _____

3 **Match the words and create collocations. Use different colours.**

1	damage	A	someone for something
2	carry	B	a threat to someone or something
3	pose	C	someone's livelihood
4	blame	D	diseases

4 **Tick (✓) three different ways in which Monty refers to the monkeys.**

the animals _____
these creatures _____
we _____
they _____

For more help with Writing Part 2: Review:
→ **Student's Book Writing bank** page 238

HOW WAS UNIT 6?

Gave it a go	☐
Needed a bit of help	☐
Getting there	☐
Aced it!	☐

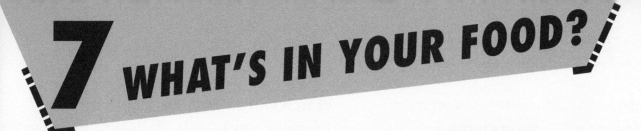

7 WHAT'S IN YOUR FOOD?

GRAMMAR

a **b**

Scan the QR codes and watch the grammar animations.

Sometimes, when talking about yourself, we use **were** not was.
Regret + verb -ing can also be used to talk about past regrets.
Wish + **person** + **would** + **infinitive** is used when someone is doing something we do not like and wish it could change.
If you think something might happen or want something to happen in the future, use hope not wish.

1 Read the texts and answer the questions.

1 **I wish my sister would clear up the kitchen after she cooks.** She spills food all over the place and I have to clear it up before Mum comes home. The food she cooks always smells great, though. I usually try to get some leftovers but there never are any. Her friends are so greedy!

Nisha (female, 18)

2 **If only I'd learnt to cook** when I had the chance! I'm at university now and I have to eat takeaways and convenience foods, which I don't really enjoy. It's also very expensive. My parents told me I should learn, but I was too busy with my exams. I should have listened to them.

Yohan (male, 20)

3 My favourite food is Japanese. It looks so elegant and it's also really healthy. The trouble is it's so expensive here. If only I **were** Japanese! I wish Japanese food was cheaper – and it would be great if they gave you a bit more in the restaurants!

Olivia (female, 22)

4 I've been studying catering at college for the last few months. I really **hope** to have a restaurant of my own one day. I want to serve fusion food – that means food which mixes different cuisines. I love cooking! I just wish I'd started the course when I was younger.

Tomasz (male, mid-30s)

1 Who regrets not following good advice?   <u>Yohan</u>

2 Who would like their favourite food to be cheaper?   _____

3 Who gets annoyed with someone else's behaviour?   _____

4 Who has food-related ambitions?   _____

2 **Read the texts again. Complete the sentences with the correct form of the verbs.**

1 Olivia **(wish)** __wishes__ she were Japanese.

2 Yohan wishes he **(learn)** _____ to cook when he was living at home.

3 Nisha **(annoy)** _____ with her sister.

4 Tomasz **(regret)** _____ not starting the course earlier.

5 Nisha wishes her sister's friends **(not be)** _____ so greedy.

3 **Match the halves of the sentences.**

1	That menu looked amazing. If I'd been there,	A	we could have eaten it now.
2	If my grandma had eaten the way we do now,	B	she wouldn't have lived to be 100.
3	If I hadn't forgotten to put the lasagne in the fridge last night,	C	I would have chosen the goat's cheese and pear salad.

4	I'd have spent less money	D	if you'd remembered to add sugar.
5	The cake would be tastier	E	we would be healthier now.
6	If we hadn't eaten so much junk food when we were young,	F	if I had gone to the market instead of the supermarket.

For more help, go to the Grammar reference:
➔ **Student's Book** pages 218–219

VOCABULARY

1 **Complete the sentences with the correct words.**

> stick to   gone off   savoury   ~~allergic~~
> in season   appetite

1 **A:** Is there anything you don't eat?
   B: Yes, shellfish. I'm __allergic__ to it.

2 Do you prefer sweet or _____ food?

3 **A:** Why are these strawberries so expensive?
   B: Because they're not _____ at the moment.

4 **A:** You haven't eaten very much.
   B: No, I've lost my _____ . I think I might be ill.

5 I tried to be a vegetarian but I couldn't _____ it for very long.

6 That meat smells terrible. I think it's _____ .

Need help? ➔ **Student's Book** page 95

2 **Write the prefixes.**

Match to the word groups.

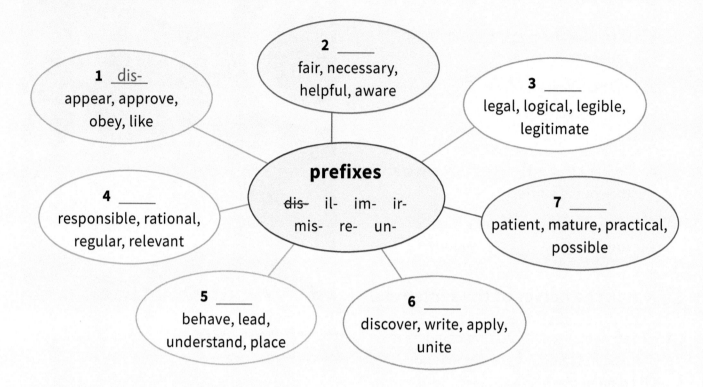

1 <u>dis-</u>
appear, approve, obey, like

2 _____
fair, necessary, helpful, aware

3 _____
legal, logical, legible, legitimate

prefixes
~~dis-~~ il- im- ir- mis- re- un-

4 _____
responsible, rational, regular, relevant

7 _____
patient, mature, practical, possible

5 _____
behave, lead, understand, place

6 _____
discover, write, apply, unite

Need help? → **Student's Book** page 99

3 **Complete the sentences with the correct words.**

dislikes   misunderstood   irresponsible
~~illegal~~   rewrite   unaware

1 A new law in the UK has made it ___illegal___ for teenagers under the age of sixteen to buy energy drinks.

2 I think he _____ me because he did the exact opposite of what I told him to do.

3 I had to _____ the whole essay as my tutor told me it was all factually incorrect.

4 I was _____ of the fact that lemons contain more sugar than strawberries until my teacher told me about it this morning.

5 I love eating broccoli but my brother really _____ it. It makes him feel sick!

6 I think it's _____ of people to throw away plastic bottles. They should try to reuse them as much as possible.

READING AND USE OF ENGLISH PART 2

! STRATEGY

- Read the text and predict the missing words.
- Highlight or <u>underline</u> the words near the space.
- Think about the missing word.
- Check your work. Do you have the correct verb forms?

For questions 1–8, read the text below and think of the word which best fits each gap. Use only one word in each gap. There is an example at the beginning (0).

We all know **(0)** __how__ successful advertising is. The adverts we remember most are probably for everyday things **(1)** _____ as soft drinks, sweets and convenience foods. We all know what we should **(2)** _____ eating – healthy food, such as fruit and vegetables. The trouble is these foods are never advertised!

So, what would happen **(3)** _____ advertisers used all their sophisticated techniques to try and sell healthy food to children? Maybe they could make vegetables seem cool and fruit the thing teenagers want to be seen eating. Most of **(4)** _____ would agree that it would be a good thing, but the trouble is farmers and fruit growers do not have enough money to spend **(5)** _____ advertising. So, who would pay **(6)** _____ it? Governments, for a start, as they would save money if people **(7)** _____ healthier. Local businesses could contribute and celebrities could be asked to give their time for free. After **(8)** _____ , everybody wants a healthier future generation.

For more help with Reading and Use of English Part 2: ➜ Student's Book Exam Focus page 90

1 🔊 12 **Listen to Sofia and Enrique deciding which type of food to have for a party. What do they decide to eat?** _____

2 **Listen again. Circle the reason for not choosing the items.**

1 a formal dinner at a restaurant
   A It's not special enough.
   Ⓑ It's too expensive.

2 everyone cooks a dish and brings it
   A It's too difficult.
   B It's too expensive.

3 tea, coffee and cake
   A It's not very healthy.
   B It's not special enough.

4 snack foods such as crisps, nuts and popcorn
   A It's not special enough.
   B It's not very healthy.

→ 🔊 **Go to page 103 to read the audioscript if you need further help.**

3 **Use colours to match what Sofia and Enrique say with a function.**

They say ...		Function	
1	What do you think?	A	agreeing
2	You've got a point.	B	making a suggestion
3	So, what about getting pizza?	C	justifying an opinion
4	It's cheap and pretty convenient.	D	asking for an opinion

5	That would be really fun.	E	giving an opinion
6	Definitely not!	F	speculating
7	It might turn out better than you think.	G	disagreeing

4 **13 Listen to four speakers. Which speaker answers each question?**

A	Can you tell me about a special meal you've had recently?	Speaker _4_
B	What kind of restaurants are popular with people in your country?	Speaker ___
C	What foods do you eat on festival days in your country?	Speaker ___
D	Do people in your country usually eat a meal with their family every day?	Speaker ___

5 13 **Listen to the speakers again. Complete the sentences with the correct words.**

~~tasty~~   stuffed   filling   desserts

1 It takes quite a long time to make, which is why it's really _tasty_ .

2 My grandma is an amazing cook and my aunts and uncles usually bring cakes and _____ , so I always enjoy Sunday lunch.

3 The food is really tasty and _____ and you can ask them to make it less spicy if you want.

4 I ate so much that I was absolutely _____ !

→ **Go to page 104 to read the audioscript if you need further help.**

Go to page 104 to read the audioscript if you need further help.

PUSH YOURSELF / C1

Circle the correct adverbs.

1 **Apparently** / **Ultimately**, they've found out that butter is good for you. They've been telling us not to eat it for years.

2 **Undoubtedly** / **Remarkably**, milk costs less than it did five years ago.

3 **Ultimately** / **Supposedly**, you have to follow the diet that suits your lifestyle and budget.

4 **Supposedly** / **Inevitably**, you lose weight if you eat very little on two days of the week.

5 **Apparently** / **Inevitably**, I gave up my diet after a week.

6 **Undoubtedly** / **Remarkably**, eating five portions of fresh fruit and vegetables every day is a good idea.

HOW WAS UNIT 7?

Gave it a go	☐
Needed a bit of help	☐
Getting there	☐
Aced it!	☐

8 LIVING MADE EASY

Scan the QR code and watch the grammar animation.

Modals of speculation and deduction	Present	Past
Certainly true	must You must be tired.	must have + past participle You must have been tired.
Certainly not true	can't He can't eat my biscuits.	can't have + past participle He can't have eaten my biscuits.
Possibly true	may / might / could She might arrive late.	may / might / could have + past participle She might have arrived late.

1 **Do the pairs of sentences have similar or different meanings?**

Circle S (similar) or D (different).

1	Connor can't have been driving the car at the time of the accident. There is a chance that Connor was driving the car at the time of the accident.	S / (D)
2	My computer suddenly stopped working – I think it might have crashed. It is possible that my computer has crashed.	S / D
3	The virus may have come from that email you opened. The virus definitely came from that email you opened.	S / D
4	There may be life on other planets. Some people believe there is life on other planets.	S / D
5	The plants have all died – she must have forgotten to water them. I believe she didn't water her plants, which is why they died.	S / D
6	Black holes might lead to other parts of the universe. It is a fact that black holes lead to other parts of the universe.	S / D
7	There must be other sources of renewable energy. There will be problems if we don't find other sources of renewable energy.	S / D

2 **Complete the sentences with one or two words including a modal verb of deduction or speculation.**

Use must, can't or may / might / could.

1 Peter _must_ **be** stuck in traffic. He's never normally late.

2 Michael lost his job last month. It _____ **been** easy for him since then.

3 I wonder why my computer isn't working properly. It _____ **be** due to the recent upgrade or perhaps there's an issue with the battery.

4 I'm not sure why I got such a low mark for my biology essay. I think I _____ **misread** the question, or perhaps it was my grammar.

5 That's my sister on the phone again. She _____ **forgotten** to tell me something the first time she rang.

6 There _____ **be** life on Mars. The aliens would have visited us by now!

Scan the QR code and watch the grammar animation.

3 **Match the halves of the sentences. Use different colours.**

1	My mother used to sing that song	A	that test tube please?
2	Can you pass me	B	to me when I was a child.
3	I can't believe they offered	C	of complaint to the manager.
4	You should write a letter	D	me the job!

5	I lent my brother	E	the electrician's phone number.
6	My auntie bought me	F	my car for a few days.
7	Arjun gave his uncle	G	a new jumper for my birthday.

4 **Circle the correct words.**

1 You need to **tell** / **tell to** me the truth.

2 Can you pour **for me** / **me** another cup of tea, please?

3 I **taught** / **taught to** them a new card game.

4 Can you do **for me** / **me** a favour?

5 The teacher read the instructions out **to** / **–** the class.

6 Leila gave **to** / **–** her cousin some good advice.

For more help, go to the Grammar reference:
→ **Student's Book** pages 220–221

PUSH YOURSELF /C1

Complete the sentences with the correct words.

> though Realistically ~~likelihood~~
> possibly appears suggests

1 In all _likelihood_ , the computer developed a virus which is why it's not working.

2 It looks as _____ the servers might have overheated.

3 Scientific evidence _____ that mobile phones can cause health problems later in life.

4 My laptop can't _____ have developed an issue. I only bought it last week.

5 It _____ that the funding has been withdrawn so we'll probably need to pull the plug on the project.

6 _____ speaking, we don't have a chance of meeting the deadline next Monday.

VOCABULARY

1 Complete the second sentence so it has a similar meaning to the first.

Use the word given.

Do not change the word given.

Use one or two words.

1 We **misunderstood** each other.

   GOT

   We ___got___ our _____ crossed.

2 Duncan has **lost his enthusiasm** for the project.

   OUT

   Duncan has run _____ _____ steam.

3 This is **very easy** to understand.

   NOT

   It is _____ _____ science.

4 Jake **loses** his **temper easily**.

   SHORT

   Jake has got _____ _____ fuse.

5 Susan **suddenly understood** English grammar.

   LIGHTBULB

   Susan had a _____ _____ and understood English grammar.

6 The company decided to **withdraw support** for the project.

   PULL

   The company decided _____ _____ the plug on the project.

Need help? → **Student's Book** page 111

2 **14 Listen to the speakers. What are they talking about? Write letters.**

A breakthroughs	D backup
B ~~spreadsheets~~	E screenshot
C upgrades	F icons

Speaker 1	B
Speaker 2	___
Speaker 3	___
Speaker 4	___
Speaker 5	___
Speaker 6	___

Need help? → **Student's Book** page 108

→ Go to page 104 to read the audioscript if you need further help.

LISTENING PART 2

(!) STRATEGY

- Read the question and <u>underline</u> the key words.
- Read the statements and think about the words you will hear.
- Make notes.
- Remember you listen twice.
- It's OK to write numbers.

15 You will hear a marine biologist called Marie Jackson talking about her work with seahorses. For questions 1–10, complete the sentences with a word or short phrase.

1 A <u>seahorse pregnancy</u> lasts for __2 to 6__ weeks. number?

2 Most <u>new-born</u> seahorses do <u>not</u> __survive__. verb?

3 When seahorse couples see each other in the morning, they do a dance and _____.

4 Marie compares the way seahorses eat to an _____.

5 Because they need lots of food, seahorses have excellent _____.

6 Marie describes seahorses as very _____ animals because they are very sensitive to injury.

7 It is particularly important for people interested in seahorses to avoid using a camera _____.

8 Some people consume seahorses as they believe it will make them _____.

9 Marie supports _____ on taking seahorses out of the oceans and selling them.

10 Those who want to help could make a note of their sightings of seahorses or even _____ a seahorse.

→ Go to page 105 to read the audioscript if you need further help.

For more help with Listening Part 2:
→ **Student's Book Exam Focus** page 103

WRITING PART 2: REPORT

1 Read the Writing Part 2 task and the sample report. Complete the gaps with words from the box. Add capital letters to the words if necessary.

A website on learning English is collecting reports from different countries on how technology is used in schools around the world.

Write a report on the use of technology to learn English in your country. You should:
- summarise the current situation
- recommend how the use of technology could be improved.

the problem is   however   findings
opinions   recommendations
introduction   the most useful thing

Using technology to learn English in South Korea

(1) <u>introduction</u>

I asked students of English in Seoul what kind of technology they use to learn English and which they think is the most useful. Altogether 17 students studying at language schools and high schools gave me their views.

(2) _____

The main finding was that every student I spoke to uses online resources and apps to practise their English. Most students shared the following **(3)** _____ :

There is plenty of online material and many suitable apps for learning English. **(4)** _____ there is not enough guidance on which are the best for different types of student and which should be avoided.

Using apps is really useful for students in their self-study time. Most learners, **(5)** _____, prefer to work in groups and engage with their teacher during class time.

(6) _____ about technology is that it is now easy to gain access to English films, songs and texts. These are even more popular than materials designed specifically for language learning.

(7) _____

Teachers should limit technology use in class and interact with students instead.

Schools should recommend the best websites and apps for students.

2 Match the words with the definitions. Use different colours.

1	altogether	A	advice or help
2	views	B	learning on your own
3	guidance	C	in total
4	self-study	D	opinions

5	engage	E	for a particular reason
6	specifically	F	restrict
7	limit	G	interact with people

3 **Match the titles to the expressions.**

Introduction
Advantages and disadvantages
Recommendations

report

The aim of this report is to ...
This report is intended to ...
The main purpose of this report
is to provide ...

I would strongly suggest that ...
This would be ideal for ...
We might want to consider ...

One of the main advantages of this is ...
The positive aspects of this are ...
One of the drawbacks to this is ...

For more help with Writing Part 2: Report:
➜ **Student's Book Exam Focus** page 242

HOW WAS UNIT 8?

Gave it a go ☐

Needed a bit of help ☐

Getting there ☐

Aced it! ☐

9 THE GREAT OUTDOORS

1 (Circle) the correct future forms.

1. In another decade, we'll all **(be wearing)** / **worn** 'smart suits' or wearable computers.

2. By the middle of the century, people **will become** / **will have become** younger instead of older.

3. It is more than likely that the buildings of the future **might be** / **will be** able to talk to us.

4. Some scientists believe that by 2040 we **will have given up** / **will be giving up** using computers.

5. In all probability, the weather **will eventually be** / **will have eventually been** controlled by humans.

6. In a few hundred years, we may no longer **be speaking** / **have spoken** English.

7. Within a few years, scientists will have **developed** / **will be developing** meat grown in laboratories.

8. In 250 million years, all the continents **will join up** / **will have joined up** into one large block of land.

2 Complete the sentences with the correct form of the future perfect or the future continuous.

1. In May, I **(work)** _will be working_ in the new library that's being built.

2. What do you think you **(achieve)** _____ in five years' time?

3. We **(watch)** _____ the big game after 8 pm.

4. By July next year, I **(finish)** _____ my course at college.

5. This time next week, we **(swim)** _____ in the sea.

3 (Circle) the correct words.

1. There is **a** / **(no)** prospect of finding life on Mars during my lifetime.

2. It is possible that researchers will **be finding** / **have found** a cure for the common cold in the near future.

3. In 200 years' time, some inhabited islands **are disappearing** / **will disappear** under the sea.

4. Will chimpanzees **be becoming** / **have become** extinct by the end of the century?

5. There's a chance that robots will **be replaced** / **have replaced** most manual workers by 2050.

For more help, go to the Grammar reference:
→ **Student's Book** pages 222–223

Complete the sentences with the correct phrases.

> counting down the days
> ~~get around to~~
> just around the corner
> sign of things to come
> sooner or later

1   I'll ___get around to___ washing the car this afternoon.

2   We'll find a solution to the problem _____ .

3   There are university courses that can be done completely online. It's a _____ .

4   I believe the day that people start using driverless cars is _____ .

5   I'm _____ until we go on holiday.

VOCABULARY

1   Complete the sentences with the correct words.

> Dense   ~~gale-force~~   heavy   violent
> bright   soaring

1   The sea is very rough because of the ___gale-force___ **winds**.

2   _____ **fog** means that driving conditions will be extremely poor.

3   The bridge has been closed due to the _____ **storms**.

4   The _____ **temperatures** have led to a water shortage in some areas.

5   The storms are set to continue with _____ **rain** predicted for most areas.

6   The clouds will move away leading to _____ **skies** in the afternoon.

2 Complete the sentences with the correct prepositions.

> ~~out~~   over   up   through   down
> up   over

1   Finally, the sun has **come** ___out___ . We can go on a picnic after all.

2   The wind seems to be **dying** _____ . I don't think we can go sailing today.

3   Oh no, it's starting to **cloud** _____ . I hope it won't rain.

4   The wind seems to be **picking** _____ again. Maybe I'll hang the clothes out to dry.

5   The pond in our village **freezes** _____ every winter. You can skate on it during the coldest months.

6   The hurricane **ripped** _____ the town, destroying everything in its path.

7   The weather seems to be **brightening** _____ . Let's go for a swim!

3 Match the words to make collocations. Use different colours.

1	glorious	A	rain
2	persistent	B	storm
3	a heavy	C	sunshine
4	a fierce	D	downpour

5	poor	E	humidity
6	stifling	F	weather
7	changeable	G	visibility

Need help? ➜ **Student's Book** page 121

4 Put the words in the correct columns in the table. Make any necessary changes.

> refer   decide   meaning   ~~hesitate~~
> accomplish   special   accurate

-ation	-ence	-ment
celebration	evidence	achievement
hesitation	_____	_____

-ist	-ful	
biologist	colourful	
_____	_____	

-ive	-acy	
competitive	privacy	
_____	_____	

5 Complete the sentences with a word from the table.

1   There is no scientific _evidence_ to suggest that life exists on other planets.

2   It was a wonderful birthday _____ . All of his friends and family were there.

3   She works as a _____ and spends a lot of her time in the lab.

4   Sending humans to Mars would be an amazing _____ .

5   My brother is really _____ . He always wants to win.

6   Satellites are able to track down our location with amazing _____ .

! STRATEGY

- Read the text.
- Look at the word before and after the gap.
- Consider what word is needed. A noun? An adjective?
- Does the word need a prefix or a suffix?
- Write the word in the space. Does it read well?

For questions 1–8, read the text below. Use the word given in capitals at the end of some of the lines to form a word that fits in the gap in the same line. There is an example at the beginning (0).

Life on board the International Space Station	
Have you ever wondered what life is like on the International Space Station?	
In many ways, it is like life on Earth but there are some major **(0)** _differences_ .	DIFFERENT
For one thing, astronauts need to exercise for at least two hours a day to	
prevent bone and muscle loss. The **(1)** _____ they use is different to	EQUIP
what we use on Earth because in space people are **(2)** _____ .	WEIGH
Another thing is that food is slightly different because there is not much	
(3) _____ space on board. Most food is dried and they are	STORE
(4) _____ to use things like salt and pepper as they will typically fly	ABLE
away! Instead they use **(5)** _____ designed liquid seasoning.	SPECIAL
What **(6)** _____ do astronauts do in their free time? They can watch	ACTIVE
films, read or play games but most enjoy looking out of the window.	
The sunrise, which occurs every 45 minutes, can be **(7)** _____ .	SPECTACLE
When they are sleeping, they have to make sure they are strapped in so that	
they cannot move. If they became **(8)** _____ , they could fly around	ATTACH
and hurt themselves.	

For more help with Reading and Use of English Part 3: ➔ **Student's Book Exam Focus page 102**

SPEAKING PART 1

1 **Read the statements about Part 1 of the Speaking test.**

Write ✓ (true) or ✗ (false).

1 In Part 1, the candidates discuss something together. ✗

2 Each candidate will be asked at least four different questions. ___

3 The questions in Part 1 are related to familiar topics. ___

4 Part 1 lasts about two minutes. ___

5 Part 1 is designed to be the most difficult. ___

2 🔊 **16 Listen to two students' answers to a Part 1 question, 'Tell us about a place you have visited in your country'.**

Circle their response.

	Honza, Czech Republic	Alicia, Spain
Name of the place	Kutná Hora	Ciudad Encantada
Why people visit	historic **buildings** / **boats**	the rocks formed into strange **shapes** / **groups**
The atmosphere of the place	**exciting** / **relaxed**	**lively** / **mysterious**
Adjectives used to describe the place	**stunning, beautiful** / **busy, crowded**	**boring** / **memorable, breathtaking, misty**
The speaker's opinion	He **would** / **wouldn't** recommend it.	It **is** / **isn't** amazing.

3 16 **Listen again. Complete the sentences with the words the speakers use.**

get the chance as beautiful as ~~which is~~ the most breathtaking have been formed

1 **Honza:** … such as the Cathedral of St. Barbara, which is really stunning!

2 **Honza:** Actually, I would say it's just __________ Prague.

3 **Honza**: If you __________, I'd definitely recommend a visit.

4 **Alicia:** The name means Enchanted City and it really is __________ place I've ever seen.

5 **Alicia:** Over many years the rocks __________ into strange shapes …

→ Go to page 106 to read the audioscript if you need further help.

Which sentence uses the grammatical structures below? Write a number.

A a passive structure 5

B a relative clause __

C a conditional sentence __

D a superlative __

E a comparative __

4 **Match the halves of the sentences. Use different colours.**

1	Last summer I visited **London**,	A	**as** in summer.
2	The countryside can be just **as** beautiful in winter	B	is one of the most beautiful **cities** in the world.
3	**If** you get the chance,	C	**which** is full of historic buildings.
4	I would say that **Istanbul**	D	**over** the last ten years.
5	The museum has been **extended**	E	**I'd** definitely **suggest** that you go there.

For more help with Speaking Part 1:

→ **Student's Book Speaking bank** pages 244–245

HOW WAS UNIT 9?

Gave it a go ☐

Needed a bit of help ☐

Getting there ☐

Aced it! ☐

GRAMMAR

Scan the QR code and watch the grammar animation.

1 Complete the second sentence so that it has a similar meaning to the first sentence.

Use the word given.

Do not change the word given.

Use between two and five words.

1 My parents **say I can't** play video games on weekdays.

   LET

   My parents _won't let me_ play video games on weekdays.

2 I **will call** Taro to see **whether he can give** you swimming lessons.

   ARRANGE

   I will _____ give you swimming lessons.

3 Geeta **needs** the coach to **repair her tennis racket**.

   GET

   Geeta has to _____ by the coach.

4 We **are forced to get up** at 5 am for training by the coach.

   MAKES

   Our coach _____ at 5 am for training.

5 I **need to finish writing my report** before the meeting.

   GET

   I must _____ before the meeting.

6 A famous fashion designer **is going to design** our new kit.

   HAVE

   We are going to _____ by a famous fashion designer.

2 Read the article and (circle) the correct words.

The Goal for Life Foundation was set up in 2011 to (**help**)/ **let** children from disadvantaged backgrounds to reach their sporting goals. The charity arranges for professional footballers **coach** / **to coach** the boys and girls for free – everyone involved is a volunteer. The regular training sessions **cause** / **let** children develop their skills in an enjoyable and supportive environment. The charity has managed to **have** / **get** local shops and restaurants to provide sports kits, equipment and meals for the students. It has been wonderful to see the community support for the Foundation. The organisers allow parents **come** / **to come** along too to offer support and encouragement to their children. The Co-ordinator of Goal for Life, Chris Roberts, said: 'It's important to **help** / **get** children interested in sports from an early age. As well as the health benefits, it **helps** / **allows** them develop self-confidence. We have also seen some wonderful friendships develop here.'

Scan the QR code and watch the grammar animation.

Adjectives with -ing and -ed

People often confuse adjectives that end in -ed, like bored or excited, with adjectives that end in -ing, for example, boring or exciting.

The difference is that:

- adjectives that end in -ed describe emotions – they tell us how people feel about something.

  e.g. Did you see that video about spiders? Yes, I was terrified by it.

- adjectives that end in -ing describe the thing that produces the feeling.

  e.g. I watched a terrifying video about spiders on YouTube.

3 Complete the sentences with the correct form of the adjectives.

1 I tried to learn how to code but I found it really **(confuse)** confusing.

2 I was **(shock)** _____ to hear that they had been eliminated from the competition.

3 I don't know about you but I find the commentator really **(irritate)** _____ .

4 We went to the new restaurant and the musicians they had there were **(amaze)** _____ .

5 Personally, I found the film **(disappoint)** _____ but I know others absolutely loved it.

6 My friends and I were really **(exhaust)** _____ after our 10 km run.

7 The fact that I had been accepted onto the programme was **(excite)** _____ .

Complete the second sentence so that it has a similar meaning to the first sentence.

1 I love hiking because of the views.

   What I love about _hiking is the views_ .

2 My brother got me interested in tennis.

   It was my brother _____ in tennis.

3 I enjoy bungee jumping because of the excitement.

   One thing _____ is the excitement.

4 I go running every day to keep fit.

   One reason _____ is to keep fit.

5 I love playing sport because of the competition.

   What I _____ is the competition.

6 Baseball is really popular in my country.

   One activity _____ in my country is baseball.

For more help, go to the Grammar reference:
→ **Student's Book** pages 224–225

VOCABULARY

1 Choose a word from the box and write it in the correct form.

> spectate   ~~decide~~   excite   impress
> separate   compete

1 The (noun – thing) _decision_ was made to cancel the match due to the poor weather.

2 The (noun – person) _____ gave the players a standing ovation as they walked onto the pitch.

3 The (noun – thing) _____ begins next week and over 100 teams have entered.

4 The fans had to be (adjective) _____ due to the fierce rivalry.

5 Everyone was singing and dancing. You could feel the (noun – thing) _____ in the stadium.

6 The fact that she was unbeaten throughout the whole tournament was really (adjective) _____ .

2 Match the words and definitions. Use different colours.

1	A person who takes part in sports, particularly in a competitive way.	A	spectators
2	A person or team who competes against you in a sports competition or debate.	B	opponent
3	People who watch a sports event but do not necessarily support one team or competitor.	C	athlete

4	The fans of a particular team or competitor.	D	audience
5	People who are watching a concert, play, film or TV show.	E	supporters
6	A person who takes part in a contest.	F	competitor

Need help? → **Student's Book** page 139

68

3 🎧 17 **Listen to two students, Jan (J) and Isabel (I).**

They answer the question: 'Should the working week be reduced from five days to four?'

(Circle) **who says the things below.**

1	Who agrees?	(J)	I
2	Who disagrees?	J	I
Who makes the following points?			
3	Technological advances make our work easier.	J	(I)
4	Computers and other devices take up more of our time.	J	I
5	People nowadays have more spare time than people did in the past.	J	I
6	Lots of people have jobs or follow courses away from the place they come from.	J	I
7	People need only a little more free time.	J	I
8	The problem of lack of time is worse for young people.	J	I

→ 🎧 Go to page 106 to read the audioscript if you need further help.

4 🎧 17 **Listen again and complete the sentences with the correct words.**

Jan

in particular	~~in comparison with~~
For example	First of all

1 I know that <u>in comparison with</u> the past we have a lot of leisure time.

2 _____, life in general is a lot busier than it was.

3 _____, we have to update our social media.

4 There's a lot of pressure on young people _____ .

Isabel

~~On balance~~	in my view	Besides
Having said that		

5 <u>On balance</u> , I feel that most of us have about the right amount of leisure time.

6 _____, for most of us work is not as hard as it was in the past.

7 _____, lots of people have to move far away from their hometown.

8 But _____, we don't need a three-day weekend every week.

Need help? → **Student's Book** page 136

→ 🎧 Go to page 106 to read the audioscript if you need further help.

SPEAKING PARTS 3 AND 4

1 🔊 19 **Read the task below. Then listen to Todd and Christina discuss the task. Which facility do they agree is the best idea?**

A cinema complex

A bowling centre

Your town has decided to spend some money on ONE of these leisure facilities.

A swimming pool

A community park

A library

2 🔊 19 **Listen again. Tick (✓) the options they discuss.**

3 🔊 19 **Listen again. Underline the discourse markers you hear.**

besides	in that case
for example	such as
<u>to be honest</u>	anyway
in comparison	I think
on balance	

→ 🔊 Go to page 107 to read the audioscripts if you need further help.

For more help with Speaking Part 3:
→ **Student's Book Speaking bank page 250**

4 **Read the Part 4 questions and the replies given by a candidate called Mai. Then answer the questions.**

1 Do you think governments should spend more money on sports and leisure facilities?

That's quite a difficult question because the government has so many things to spend money on. Some people might say that there are more important things than <u>tennis courts</u> and running tracks – (for example,) hospitals and schools. However, in my view, we shouldn't underestimate the value of all types of leisure, not just sports. I mean, people are more likely to get sick if they don't have enough relaxation and that could cost more money in the long run.

a Does the candidate answer the question?

b What is her opinion?

c (Circle) the discourse markers she uses.

d <u>Underline</u> the sports and leisure-related vocabulary she uses.

2 Do you think sports should be compulsory in schools?

Well, this might be an unpopular view, but no, I don't. For me, when you force people to do something, that thing becomes less attractive to them. The aim of schools should be to get young people to develop a lifelong love of sports and exercise. So, what they need to do is let students choose whether to do sports or not, and then make it fun and not too competitive so that even those who are not naturally sporty want to take part.

a Does the candidate answer the question?

b What is her opinion?

c (Circle) the discourse markers she uses.

d <u>Underline</u> the sports and leisure-related vocabulary she uses.

For more help with Speaking Part 4:
→ **Student's Book Speaking bank page 252**

LISTENING PART 3

1 🎧 **18 You will hear five short extracts in which people are talking about an activity they do during their leisure time.**

For questions 1–5, choose from the list (A–H) one disadvantage of the activity that the speaker mentions. Use the letters only once. There are three extra letters which you do not need to use.

A	The activity can be <u>expensive</u>.	**Speaker 1** C
B	There is a <u>danger</u> of getting <u>hurt</u>.	**Speaker 2** ___
C	A <u>good fitness</u> level is <u>needed</u>.	**Speaker 3** ___
D	It can be very time-consuming.	**Speaker 4** ___
E	People take competitions too seriously.	**Speaker 5** ___
F	You have to buy a lot of equipment.	
G	It's too mentally challenging.	
H	Men and women are treated differently.	

➔ 🎧 Go to page 107 to read the audioscript if you need further help.

2 Check your answers to Exercise 1.

Do these extracts help you find the answers or distract you from them?

Write A (answer) or D (distractor) for each one.

Speaker 1

1 It's true you need a lot of equipment, but most people hire it. <u>D</u>

2 Even for recreational diving, you do have to be quite fit. ___

3 … diving as a hobby is not nearly as risky as people think. ___

Speaker 2

4 You also need to be a risk-taker because injury is always a possibility. ___

5 Some equipment is used only by men, some only by women and some by both. ___

For more help with Listening Part 3:
➔ **Student's Book Exam Focus** page 77

HOW WAS UNIT 10?

Gave it a go	⌞⌝
Needed a bit of help	⌞⌝
Getting there	⌞⌝
Aced it!	⌞⌝

11 FACT OR FICTION?

Scan the QR codes and watch the grammar animations.

a   b

Reported speech
Remember tense changes we make:
present simple ➔ past simple **is** ➔ **was**
present continuous ➔ past continuous **is** going ➔ **was** going
present perfect ➔ past perfect **have** been ➔ **had** been
past simple ➔ past perfect **went** ➔ **had gone**
will ➔ **would**
Questions in reported speech We change the word order in the question to the same as a normal sentence. We make the same **tense changes** as in reported speech. We use the same **question words** (when, how, etc.). We use a full stop (.), not a question mark (?). ➔ She asked me **where** I **got** my news from. We use if or whether with Yes/No questions. ➔ She asked me **whether** I **enjoyed** watching football.

1 Look at the sentences with reported speech.

Circle said or asked.

1	Harry: 'People listened to the radio much more in my day.'	Harry (said) / asked (that) people had listened to the radio much more in his day.
2	Sophie: 'We're going to see Dream Girls at the theatre next Thursday.'	Sophie said / asked (that) they were going to see Dream Girls at the theatre the following Thursday.
3	Alain: 'What kind of news stories do you like to read?'	Alain said / asked (me) what kind of news stories I liked to read.
4	Teacher: 'Have you ever taken part in a play before?'	The teacher said / asked (me) whether I had taken part in a play before.

5	Carlos: 'My sister can sing really well but I'm a hopeless singer.'	Carlos said / asked (that) his sister could sing really well but that he was a hopeless singer.
6	The article: 'The Shape of Water was directed by Guillermo del Toro.'	The article said / asked (that) The Shape of Water had been directed by Guillermo del Toro.
7	Leyla: 'If there's an action film showing, I'll come with you to the cinema.'	Leyla said / asked (that) she would come to the cinema (with us) if there was an action film showing.

2 Complete the sentences.

> suggested   threatened   ~~criticised~~
> denied   promised   explained
> refused

1 My parents always _criticised_ **me for spending too much time** watching TV.

2 My dad _____ **to turn off the internet connection** if I didn't do my homework.

3 Patrick _____ **to arrange** some brilliant entertainment for my party.

4 Mr Wyatt _____ **to help us rehearse** for the talent show because it would give us an unfair advantage.

5 Andy _____ **giving Wendy** the best part because she was his cousin – he said it was because she was the best dancer.

6 Someone _____ **having the party** on a boat but I was against the idea.

7 Ben _____ **why** he didn't enjoy the show.

3 Circle the correct words.

1 He **said** / **told** me he would meet me after the show.

2 She asked me where **we got** / **did we get** the costumes for the school play.

3 The man who ran the theatre asked whether I **can** / **could** sing.

4 One of my friends suggested **we going** / **we went** to the opera for a change.

5 Al **told the DJ to play a different song** / **told to play a different song the DJ**.

6 Julie asked whether **had we read** / **we had read** the article.

For more help, go to the Grammar reference:
→ **Student's Book** pages 226–227

VOCABULARY

1 Circle the correct words.

1 When they developed the concept of the show, their target **audience** / **influence** was teenagers, but they later found that a lot of adults watched it too.

2 They organised a big media campaign to **embrace** / **promote** the show, but the viewing figures were really low, so they pulled the plug on it.

3 The government is taking action against social media sites which, they argue, have too much **influence** / **reality** on what people think.

4 A lot of the articles they publish in their newspaper aren't **credible** / **reality** as they don't do any background research on the facts.

5 The number of people who read articles online instead of in newspapers is **needed** / **predicted** to grow in the future.

6 The number of **spectators** / **viewers** watching the show increased dramatically during the second series.

7 The radio show failed to **attract** / **welcome** a big enough audience so they ended up cancelling it.

2 **Match the words and make collocations. Use different colours.**

1	go	**A**	time
2	brand	**B**	viral
3	prime	**C**	censorship
4	reality	**D**	privacy
5	invasion of	**E**	awareness
6	media	**F**	shows

Now match the collocations to quotations 1–5. There is one you do not need.

1 That clip was shared so widely that I think everyone on social media saw it. go viral

2 I love watching TV programmes about people's lives – they are so entertaining. _____

3 The best programmes are usually on at around 8 to 10 pm, when lots of people will be watching TV. _____

4 I think young people nowadays have a good knowledge of companies and what they make. _____

5 The biggest problem with being famous is that journalists never leave you in peace. _____

Need help? → **Student's Book** page 145

PUSH YOURSELF /C1

Complete the sentences with the correct words.

| All things In light It speaks |
| on the assumption Regardless of |

1 It speaks for itself that many TV companies charge more for advertising during prime-time hours.

2 _____ considered, social media has given people more access to news from around the world.

3 _____ of the new rules that ban junk food advertising on TV, the number of teenagers eating fast food has decreased.

4 _____ the fact that it can damage your eyes, the number of hours people spend in front of a screen has increased dramatically.

5 The newspaper has started to invest more money in improving its website _____ that more people will use it in the future.

WRITING PART 1: ESSAY

1 Read the Writing Part 1 question and model essay.

Tick (✓) the option that best reflects the writer's own idea.

A   celebrities' influence on teenagers

B   celebrities' wealth

> Some celebrities are paid huge sums of money to entertain us. Do you think this is reasonable?
>
> **Notes**
>
> Write about:
>
> 1. celebrities' loss of privacy
>
> 2. celebrities without talent
>
> 3. … (your own idea)

We have all seen photos of celebrities' luxury yachts and flashy cars. The wealth of the stars is clearly visible in fashion magazines and the
4 tabloids. In my view, **this** is totally unnecessary and creates negative values in society.

Some may say that famous people deserve their millions because their lives are no longer
8 their own. **They** are followed everywhere by photographers. But this happens only because they are so rich. We would be less interested if they wore cheap clothes and drove ordinary cars.

Only a small proportion of well-known people actually have talent. The internet has made more people than ever recognisable and allowed them to make money from their fame. These 'fake celebrities' definitely don't deserve to be so well paid.

When young people observe the huge
20 fortunes actors and singers have, **they** tend to undervalue ordinary jobs, such as being a
22 nurse or a teacher. **These** used to be the ones children aspired to, but now they just want to be rich and famous.

Overall, I believe 'stars' should be paid a moderate amount of money, just like the rest of us.

2 The writer achieves coherence by using lexical groups.

Put the words and phrases into the correct column.

> ~~wealth~~   ~~well-known~~   ~~ordinary cars~~
> ~~teacher~~   ~~celebrities~~   ~~make money~~
> huge fortunes   famous people
> flashy cars   recognisable   millions
> actors   well paid   the stars   singers
> rich   nurse   cheap clothes

Money	Fame
wealth	well-known
make money	celebrities
Possessions	**Jobs**
ordinary cars	teacher

3 Read the model answer again.

Use colours to match the pink words with what they refer to.

1	this (line 4)	A	famous people
2	They (line 8)	B	(ordinary) jobs
3	they (line 20)	C	young people
4	These (line 22)	D	the wealth of the stars

For more help with Writing Part 1: Essay
→ **Student's Book Writing Bank:** page 234

READING AND USE OF ENGLISH PART 5

! STRATEGY

- Read the questions first.
- Draw a line between options A, B, C and D.
- Predict the answer.
- Read the text, one paragraph at a time.
- <u>Underline</u> the information that matches the question.
- Circle the answer A, B, C or D.

You are going to read an extract from a novel in which a girl called Raquel takes part in a play at her local drama club. For questions 1–6, choose the answer (A, B, C or D) which you think fits best according to the text.

1 Why did Raquel think she was ideal for the part of Shirley?

   A   She was used to acting in musicals.

   (B)   She thought she matched the description of Shirley in the book.

   C   Shirley was the only female character in the play.

   D   Jodie wasn't able to sing.

2 According to the second paragraph, how do Raquel's feelings change?

   A   She feels even more upset about not getting the part.

   B   She develops feelings of jealousy towards Jodie.

   C   She becomes frustrated that Jodie can't learn her lines.

   D   She begins to accept that Jodie was right for the part.

3 Why does Raquel describe the summer in paragraph 3?

   A   to show she was no longer disappointed about the play

   B   to show what a good director Matthew was

   C   to emphasise that Jodie was missing out on the fun

   D   to demonstrate that she had made new friends

4 How did Raquel feel when she heard that Jodie's father wanted to talk to her?

   A   annoyed because she was busy doing her hair

   B   hopeful that Jodie would not be able to play Shirley

   C   worried that something was wrong

   D   scared in case he was angry with her

5 In the final paragraph, what does 'them' refer to?

   A   the other parts in the play

   B   Shirley's words

   C   the other actors

   D   the audience

6 At the end of the extract, Raquel's attitude could be described as

   A   arrogant

   B   pessimistic

   C   modest

   D   frustrated

For more help with Reading and Use of English: Part 5 → Student's Book Exam Focus page 51

I had truly believed I would get the part of Shirley. To say I was devastated that it was given to Jodie would have been an understatement. I had been convinced that I was in every way more suited to the part than she was. My long, dark hair and athletic build were much more similar to the character described in the novel than Jodie's classic blond good looks. And this was a musical – Shirley had to sing and that was another reason I should have got the part. To make matters worse, I'd just been asked to play one of Shirley's friends. Apart from the role of Shirley, the other main parts were for males, but that didn't bother me. I'd have happily put on a false beard, but no, all the other important parts had gone to the boys.

Rehearsals went on for eight weeks over the hottest part of the summer. At first, I'll confess, I wanted Jodie to fail, but as time went by I had to admit she wasn't bad. I think she must have taken some singing lessons since our previous production. She certainly had a better memory than I did. I struggled with my lines, whereas she always had hers perfectly memorised. It occurred to me that that might be why I hadn't got a bigger part. Even in the theatre, looks aren't everything, I realised.

That summer was more enjoyable than I'd expected it to be. Our director, Matthew, made the rehearsals fun, bringing us ice-cream and telling us stories about his time as a professional actor. All the actors got on well – after rehearsal, we'd hang out together in the park or at the beach. Gradually, I started having a good time. At least I could spend my evenings relaxing with the crowd instead of learning my lines.

I was at home when the call came. It was the night before the play was due to open and I was doing my hair in my room. My mum called up the stairs that Jodie's dad, Duncan Parsons, was on the line. I ran downstairs and picked up the phone, my heart racing. Why was Jodie's dad calling me on the landline? Jodie always called my mobile. Perhaps something really bad had happened! Mr Parsons told me Jodie had fallen off her bike on the way home. She was going to be fine but she had injured her shoulder.

The thoughts were racing round my head. The play was opening tomorrow night and Jodie was supposed to be playing the lead! Would we cancel the play? Could someone else take the part? Poor Jodie! How was she feeling? Suddenly, I realised that Mr Parsons was still talking.

'What was that, Mr Parsons?', I asked.

'Jodie wants you to play Shirley', he repeated.

'Me? W-w-why m-m-me?', I stammered.

'She said you knew the part', he replied.

So, that's how I came to play Shirley. I must have somehow picked up the lines during rehearsals. I knew them without realising it. Everyone clapped and cheered as we took our final bow but I'm sure Jodie would have been a better Shirley than me.

HOW WAS UNIT 11?

Gave it a go	☐
Needed a bit of help	☐
Getting there	☐
Aced it!	☐

GRAMMAR

Scan the QR code and watch the grammar animation.

1 Look at the notices. For each one, tick (✓) the TWO sentences which match the meaning of the notice.

1
> FESTIVAL ENTRY FEE: £5.00
> NO CHANGE GIVEN
> (CARDS ACCEPTED)

A You **should have** the exact money if you want to pay cash. ✓
B It's **possible** to pay by card. ✓
C It's **compulsory** to pay by card.

2
> **STRICTLY OVER 18s ONLY**
> **IN THE RESTAURANT**
> **AFTER 8 pm**

A Parents **mustn't bring their** children to the restaurant after 8 pm.
B Children **are not permitted** in the restaurant before 8 pm.
C To eat in the restaurant after 8 pm you **have to be** over 18.

3
> FESTIVAL OF FLOWERS
> RECOMMENDED DONATION:
> £3.50 PER ADULT

A All adults **are obliged** to pay £3.50.
B You **ought to** give a donation.
C It's **not compulsory** to give a donation.

4
> **FIREWORKS FORBIDDEN**
> **IN THE PARK**

A You **must not** take fireworks to the park.
B Bringing fireworks to the park is **not essential**.
C Visitors to the park **are not allowed** to bring fireworks with them.

5
> **DINNER INVITATION**
> **(TIES OPTIONAL)**

A It's **not advisable** to wear a tie.
B It's **not compulsory** to wear a tie.
C You **don't have to** wear a tie.

6
> **KEEP OFF THE GRASS**

A You do **not need to** walk on the grass.
B You **must not** walk on the grass.
C You **should not** walk on the grass.

Scan the QR code and watch the grammar animation.

2 **Complete the second sentence so that it has a similar meaning to the first sentence.**

Use the word in brackets.

1	That was not the right thing to do.	You **(ought)** <u>oughtn't to have done</u> that.
2	Let's climb that hill – we will have a good view of the ceremony from there.	Let's climb that hill – we **(able)** _____ _____ see the ceremony well from there.
3	We had to pay double for our tickets because we booked so late.	If we had booked early, we wouldn't **(needed)** _____ _____ pay double for our tickets.
4	I managed to see all my favourite bands at the festival.	I **(able)** _____ _____ all my favourite bands at the festival.
5	It would have been better to include children's films at the film festival.	They **(should)** _____ _____ children's films at the film festival.
6	Talking is not permitted during the ceremony.	Visitors **(must)** _____ _____ during the ceremony.
7	Participation in the events is not compulsory.	You **(have)** _____ _____ in the events.

For more help, go to the Grammar reference:
→ **Student's Book** pages 228–229

Re-write the sentences below in the tenses in brackets.

1 All guests must show their invitations on the door.

(FUTURE) <u>All guests will need to show their invitations on the door.</u>

2 We might be able to catch the last few minutes.

(PAST) We _____

_____ .

3 You can't take food into the arena.

(FUTURE) You _____

_____ .

4 You should bring your identity card with you.

(PAST) You _____

_____ .

5 They can book their tickets via the app.

(FUTURE) They _____

_____ .

VOCABULARY

1 Use the word given in capitals to form a word that fits in the gap in the same line.

Edinburgh Festivals

Every year in August, Scotland's capital city plays host to two festivals: the Edinburgh International Festival and the Edinburgh Fringe.

So, what's the difference?

To perform at the Edinburgh Festival you need an (1) invitation from the organisers. These are only given to **(2) exceptional** musicians, singers or theatre companies. If you attend the main festival, you will have the opportunity to see an **(3)_____** range of concerts and plays.

INVITE

EXCEPT

IMPRESS

Performers at the Fringe are not invited but they turn up (4)_____. Whereas the main festival is a serious event with ballets, operas and plays, the Fringe is a **(5)_____** mix of comedy and shows put on by amateurs.

REGARD

DELIGHT

There are no formal (6)_____ for taking part: just come along! Every year a few **(7)_____** will be talent-spotted at the Fringe and given the chance to join a top theatre company or orchestra.

REQUIRE

HOPE

Although you rarely have to pay more than a few pounds to attend a Fringe show, it is actually more **(8)_____** than the main Festival!

PROFIT

Need help? → **Student's Book** page 162

2 Choose a phrasal verb from the box to replace the underlined word or phrase in each sentence. Put the verb into the correct form.

> ~~look after~~   miss out on   dress up in
> come up against   get into   turn down
> ~~put on~~   go ahead

1   Who's <u>taking care of</u> the wedding arrangements?

    <u>look after</u>

2   In my last year at school, we <u>performed</u> a Shakespeare play.

    <u>put on</u>

3   I love <u>wearing</u> sparkly costumes at the carnival each year.

    _____

4   When we arranged the local festival, we <u>faced</u> many obstacles.

    _____

5   OK, since we all think we should have Mum's 60th birthday party at Chessington Manor, we should <u>proceed</u> and book it.

    _____

6   If we don't get our tickets early, we might <u>lose the chance to see</u> the best bands.

    _____

7   After going to the festival, I really <u>started to enjoy</u> rap music.

    _____

8   My sister was invited to take part in the May Queen pageant but she <u>declined</u> the offer.

    _____

Need help? → **Student's Book** page 161

3 Complete the article with the correct words.

upcoming accessible ~~appeal~~ publicise ~~reputation~~ unique
~~venues~~ host volunteer

Festivals have changed a lot in recent years. Whereas in the past the **(1)** _appeal_
was mainly to young people, they are increasingly attracting a wider range of attendees.
Music festivals, in particular, had a **(2)** _reputation_ for being uncomfortable events held
in muddy fields. There is now a diverse range of **(3)** _venues_ from parks and gardens
to stately homes and exhibition centres.

Festival organisers are more and more aware of the need for their event to be
(4) _____ to everyone, including all age groups and people with disabilities. The
improved reputation of festivals means that more places are willing to **(5)** _____
them, particularly as they are more likely to be profitable. Another boost for the
popularity of festivals has come from the internet. It is now much easier and cheaper
to **(6)** _____ your event to people all over the world, via social media for example.
Also, the increased competitiveness of the job market means that many young people
are willing to **(7)** _____ to work at festivals, just to have the experience on their CVs.

In addition to the most common music-based festivals, we are seeing some
(8) _____ festivals appear on the scene. The garlic festival on the Isle of Wight in the
UK, for example, celebrates this item of food and is a fun family day out. Check on the
internet or in your local newspaper to find **(9)** _____ festivals near you.

Need help? → **Student's Book** page 161

! STRATEGY

- Read the questions before you listen.
- Highlight or <u>underline</u> the key words in each question.
- Draw lines to separate A, B and C.
- Use the audioscript to help if necessary.

🔊 20 **You will hear a man called Paul Fenton being interviewed about his job as a film festival organiser. For questions 1–7, choose the best answer (A, B or C).**

1   According to Paul, <u>why</u> has a <u>job</u> like his <u>become necessary?</u>
Ⓐ   More people want to go to specialised film festivals.

B   More people visit the well-known film festivals.

C   Film festivals have become more international.

2   What does Paul say about the Brief Encounters film festival?
   A   It shows films relating to current issues.
   B   It is an example of a specialist film festival.
   C   It is a festival based in one city.

3   What advice does Paul give on choosing a type of festival?
   A   Decide whether it will be an annual event.
   B   Look into different funding options.
   C   Find out what local people are interested in.

4   In Paul's view, why did the Fantasm festival end?
   A   because audiences lost interest in the genre
   B   because of a lack of films in the genre
   C   because the organisers started to include less specialised films

5   Paul feels that most people who plan a film festival for the first time
   A   don't have a clear idea of what they want to do.
   B   realise it will take a year to plan it.
   C   think it will take less time than it does.

6   Paul can give advice to new organisers on
   A   legal, organisational and advertising issues.
   B   deciding on the theme of the festival.
   C   only the venues and the advertising campaign.

7   Overall, what does Paul consider the main purpose of his job?
   A   advising on government regulations relating to film festivals
   B   offering his clients comprehensive advice
   C   hiring the right staff on behalf of his clients

→ 🔊 **Go to page 108 to read the audioscript if you need further help.**

For more help with Listening Part 4:
→ **Student's Book Exam Focus page 168**

1 Read the exam task below.

You have received this email from your friend Nat, who is planning to visit you in your home town.

From: Nat
Re: Festival

Hi

As you suggested, my parents and I have managed to book our holiday to coincide with the local festival in your town. We are really excited! Could you let us know a bit about it and give us some advice on what to bring, what to wear, etc.?

Write your email.

Now read the answer on the right written by a student called Serena.

Some of the vocabulary could be more interesting.

Replace the underlined words and phrases with a word or phrase from the box.

Write the numbers.

1 scorching   2 only takes place
3 stunning   4 a bit tricky
5 is a huge range of
6 all this is accompanied by
7 a blast   8 huge mansions

2 The email in Exercise 1 uses a good range of sentence structures and cohesive devices. Find examples of the structures below the email.

For more help with Writing Part 2: Email:

→ **Student's Book Writing bank** page 236

Hi Nat

I was really excited to get your email this morning. I thought flights might be <u>hard</u> ☐4 to get at that time, so it's great you managed to book some.

To tell you something about the festival, it's called Los Patios and it <u>is only on</u> ☐2 here in Córdoba. The main thing is that you can see all the private gardens that are normally closed to the public. There <u>are a lot of</u> ☐5 <u>beautiful</u> ☐ displays, from <u>big houses</u> ☐ to apartments. What they have in common is that they are colourful and creative and the owners are really proud of them. As this is the south of Spain, <u>there's also</u> ☐ lots of eating, music and dancing, so prepare to have <u>a good time</u> ☐!

Regarding what to bring, there are two important things: your camera – or a phone with a good camera – and walking shoes as you will be doing a lot of walking. The weather can be <u>very hot</u> ☐ in May, so bring light cotton clothes and sun cream.

See you soon!

Serena

1 phrases to introduce answers to the questions in the task

2 modal auxiliary verbs

3 adjective + preposition

4 verb + infinitive

5 a phrase to highlight importance

6 the future continuous

7 the passive voice

HOW WAS UNIT 12?

Gave it a go ☐

Needed a bit of help ☐

Getting there ☐

Aced it! ☐

GRAMMAR

Scan the QR code and watch the grammar animation.

1 Two of the answers to each question are correct, one is not.

(Circle) the **incorrect** answer.

1 What does your brother **look like**?
   A He's tall with curly brown hair.
   B He looks a bit like me.
   C He looks like handsome.

2 What do you **feel like** doing this evening?
   A I like playing football.
   B I feel like going out for a nice meal.
   C I'm not sure. What do you want to do?

3 What does James **do**?
   A He works as an assistant to the managing director.
   B He's an accounts manager.
   C He works like a fashion designer.

4 What is your new boss **like**?
   A She's really nice – kind and very funny.
   B I don't like her. She treats me as an idiot.
   C Awful. She treats me like her servant.

5 What does his new single **sound like**?
   A It sounds brilliant.
   B It sounds like fantastic.
   C It sounds a bit like his early songs.

2 Complete the second sentence so that it has a similar meaning to the first sentence.

Use the word in brackets.

1	My brother is a software engineer for a big IT firm.	My brother **(works)** works as a software engineer for a big IT firm.
2	My aunt thinks that I am a child. It's so annoying.	My aunt **(treats)** _____ child. It's so annoying.
3	My sister and I are so alike. People think we're twins.	My sister **(just)** _____ me. People think we're twins.
4	I can tell that you've had a lot of fun today.	It **(looks)** _____ you've had a lot of fun today.
5	They heard what they thought was a loud cheer coming from inside the building.	They heard **(sounded)** _____ a loud cheer coming from inside the building.

Scan the QR code and watch the grammar animation.

3 **Do the pairs of sentences have similar or different meanings?**
Circle S (similar) or D (different).

1	You shouldn't have bought those jeans without trying them on.	
	It's good that you tried on those jeans before you bought them.	S / Ⓓ
2	I needn't have tried on so many hats as I ended up buying the first one I tried.	
	I wasted my time trying on more hats after I'd found the right one.	S / D
3	I wouldn't have bought a car from that dealer if I'd read the online reviews.	
	The dealer had bad reviews online but I didn't see that until after I'd bought the car.	S / D
4	You didn't really need to wear a suit to that event but you looked good.	
	The event required men to wear suits and you looked good in the one you wore.	S / D
5	What you should have done was to have talked to the manager immediately.	
	You didn't talk to the manager immediately but that would have been the right thing to do.	S / D
6	Sabrina needn't have ordered so many flowers – one bunch would have been enough.	
	Sabrina ordered only one bunch of flowers because that was all she needed.	S / D

For more help, go to the Grammar reference:
→ **Student's Book** pages 230–231

VOCABULARY

1 Complete the sentences with the correct words.

> ~~purchase~~ spree bargain ~~auction~~
> vlogger outfits imports industry
> campaign consumers

1 I think the most expensive _purchase_ I've ever made was when I bought a brand new car.

2 I've never actually won an online ___auction___ . Once the price goes too high, I give up.

3 I got an amazing _____ last week – a new camera at half-price!

4 I think that most _____ shop for clothes online rather than going into shops.

5 I always go on a big shopping _____ as soon as I get paid every month.

6 Julia Smith is a famous _____ who always has some really useful shopping tips when I watch her videos online.

7 I have loads of old _____ that don't fit me anymore so I'm going to donate them to charity.

8 My country _____ a lot of fruit and vegetables from abroad which means you can buy most things all year round.

9 The company has hired a famous basketball player for its new marketing _____ .

10 I used to work in the fashion _____ before setting up my own company.

Need help? → **Student's Book** page 178

2 🔊 21 Listen to Marc and Julia talking about a shopping trip.

Circle the correct words.

1 Julia / **Marc** is planning to spend some money.

2 Julia and Marc **have been** / **have never been** shopping together before.

3 Marc has **more** / **less** money than usual.

4 The last time he went shopping Marc **didn't buy much** / **spent too much**.

5 Julia **seems to know** / **doesn't seem to know** Marc very well.

3 🔊 21 Listen again and complete the phrases with the correct words.

> ~~window shopping~~ empty-handed
> shopping spree designer brands
> budget shop around bargains
> overspend

1 … maybe do a little ___window shopping___ .

2 … I was thinking of hunting out a few _____.

3 … a little look around the shops always turns into a _____.

4 I'm on a very tight _____ at the moment.

5 I know how you love your _____.

6 … if you're willing to _____ a bit.

7 … I'm sure you're not going to come home _____.

8 … but I'm not going to _____ like I did last time.

→ 🔊 Go to page 109 to read the audioscript if you need further help.

READING AND USE OF ENGLISH PART 4

! **STRATEGY**

- Draw lines to separate the questions.
- Make sure the two sentences mean the same thing.
- Read the instructions.
- Only write between two and five words (contractions count as two words).
- Spend some extra time on this part as it is worth more.
- Write as much as you can. You still get points for incomplete answers.
- Look at the example.

For questions 1–6, complete the second sentence so that it has a similar meaning to the first sentence. Use the word given.

Do not change the word given.

You must use between two and five words, including the word given. There is an example at the beginning (0).

For more help with Reading and Use of English Part 4: → **Student's Book Exam Focus page 76**

0 Kathy's clothes **are always more fashionable than** Jackson's.

AS

Jackson's clothes ___are never as___ ___fashionable as___ Kathy's.

1 The student copied the idea from a famous designer but he didn't get caught.

AWAY

The student _____ _____ the idea from a famous designer.

2 Children should always obey their parents.

AS

Children should always _____ them.

3 Do you want to go to that new shopping centre today?

FEEL

Do you _____ that new shopping centre today?

4 Sadly, I don't know much about the new design proposal.

UNFAMILIAR

Sadly, _____ the new design proposal.

5 Seeing John at the party was a surprise.

EXPECT

I _____ John at the party.

6 You always force me into watching football every weekend.

MAKE

You always _____ football every weekend.

1 🎧 22 **Look at the Part 2 Speaking task below.**

Listen to a student called Hamid doing the task.

(Circle) **the things he says, A or B.**

Why do you think the people are enjoying shopping in these situations?

1 A Hamid starts by talking about Picture 1.

   (B) Hamid starts with ideas that relate to both pictures.

2 A Hamid then moves on to talk about each picture individually.

   B Hamid continues to talk about both pictures.

3 A Hamid spends about the same amount of time on each picture.

   B Hamid talks more about Picture 1 than about Picture 2.

4 A Hamid mostly just describes what he can see in the photos.

   B Hamid uses modals to suggest ideas related to the photos.

5 A Hamid gives his opinion of the markets.

   B Hamid sticks to the facts.

6 A He ends by talking about Picture 2.

   B He ends with his opinion of what the markets have in common.

→ 🎧 Go to page 109 to read the audioscript if you need further help.

2 🔊 **22 Listen again. Complete the sentences with the exact words Hamid uses.**

> ~~appear~~ looks probably seem
> could might looks like

1 I think they are both enjoying themselves because they don't ___appear___ to be in a hurry at all.

2 … the lady is choosing some food – it _____ fruit.

3 That's _____ one reason why she's enjoying it.

4 … I think the food _____ very fresh…

5 … it _____ be locally grown and organic.

6 The things on sale _____ to be second hand…

7 … or _____ be antiques.

➔ 🔊 **Go to page 109 to read the audioscript if you need further help.**

For more help with Speaking Part 2:
➔ **Student's Book Speaking bank page 246**

Disagreeing politely. Complete the expressions with the correct words.

> ~~more a case of~~ not always the case
> don't see eye to eye   agree to disagree
> the way I see it   don't see it like that

1 Isn't it ___more a case of___ people spending too much money?

2 I'm afraid I just _____.

3 Actually, that's _____.

4 I guess we'll just have to _____.

5 I think it's clear that we _____.

6 That's not quite _____.

HOW WAS UNIT 13?

Gave it a go	⌐⌐
Needed a bit of help	⌐⌐
Getting there	⌐⌐
Aced it!	⌐⌐

14 NOT JUST 9-5

Scan the QR code and watch the grammar animation.

1 Match the sentences to a more emphatic sentence.

Use different colours.

1	You **need to** log on to our website and complete the application form.	A	**What** I feel is that most companies still don't give employees enough time off.
2	You **must not** reveal the plans for the new products to anyone.	B	**It's only when** you start working full-time that you realise how easy student life is.
3	You **realise** how easy student life is when you start working full-time.	C	**What** you need to do is log on to our website and complete the application form.
4	I **feel** that most companies **still don't give** employees **enough time off**.	D	**Under no circumstances** must you reveal the plans for the new products to anyone.
5	Isla runs her own company **and** works as a volunteer at the local hospital.	E	**Never** have I worked with such annoying people.
6	**This is the first time** I've worked with such annoying people!	F	**What** I find frustrating is that you can only get a job if you have experience already.
7	I find it frustrating **that** you can only get a job if you have experience already.	G	**Not only** does Isla run her own company **but** she **also** works as a volunteer at the local hospital.

2 (Circle) the correct words.

1 I **have known** / **have been knowing** Jessica for almost five years.

2 I avoid **to eat** / **eating** food which contains nuts because I'm allergic.

3 I've been working at the hospital for six months but I'm still **being** / **getting** used to the early starts.

4 **Provided** / **Unless** he passes his final exam, Simon will start university in the autumn.

5 We **didn't even finish** / **hadn't even finished** our starters when, suddenly, the main course turned up.

6 They **prevented** / **warned** us against travelling on the roads due to the poor weather conditions.

3 (Circle) **the correct answer.**

1 I really regret not _____ computer programming at school as it's such a useful skill to have nowadays.
   A to study
   (B) studying

2 The restaurant's always fully booked. The food there _____ be really good.
   A can't
   B must

3 It doesn't look like the engineers _____ the issue in time for the start of the concert.
   A will have fixed
   B will be fixing

4 The tour guide will let us _____ the tour, provided we pay the full amount in advance.
   A join
   B to join

5 The manager _____ to give me a refund even though I had a receipt.
   A denied
   B refused

6 It isn't _____ to make a donation but you can if you want to.
   A compulsory
   B permitted

7 I _____ that last piece of cake. I feel really sick now.
   A needn't have eaten
   B shouldn't have eaten

8 Under no circumstances _____ speak during the exam.
   A you must
   B must you

For more help, go to the Grammar reference:
➔ **Student's Book** page 232

VOCABULARY

1 🔊 **23 Listen to six people talking. Write their jobs.**

| financial advisor   air traffic controller |
| children's entertainer   freelance consultant |
| property developer   ~~pharmacist~~ |

Speaker 1   __pharmacist__

Speaker 2   _____

Speaker 3   _____

Speaker 4   _____

Speaker 5   _____

Speaker 6   _____

➔ 🔊 **Go to page 110 to read the audioscript if you need further help.**

2 Complete the sentences with the correct words.

> redundant ~~freelance~~ expenses
> sack application notice
> promotion vacancy

1 I'm thinking of going ___freelance___ as I like the idea of being my own boss.

2 I am writing to submit my _____ for the job of receptionist.

3 It's a good idea to find another job before you hand in your _____ .

4 The car factory had to make a quarter of the workforce _____ because there wasn't enough work.

5 Our company has very strict rules about how much you can claim on _____ when you go on a business trip.

6 You will need to work long hours if you want to get a _____ .

7 It's not as easy as it used to be to give someone the _____ as there are laws to protect workers.

8 I would love to work for Greyson's but they don't have a _____ at the moment.

Need help? → **Student's Book** page 190

3 Match sentences which have the same meaning. Use different colours.

1	Could you possibly set it up?	A	I haven't had time to examine the issue.
2	The comment has now been taken down from the website.	B	It might be worth asking him to look at it.
3	I haven't got round to analysing the problem yet.	C	We have removed the message from the page.
4	Why don't you run this report by the consultant?	D	It would be great if you could organise it.

5	They've put the meeting back by a week.	E	The head of the organisation wants to increase the size of the company.
6	Let me get back to you later today.	F	It's vital that we reduce our travel costs.
7	The CEO is looking into expanding the company.	G	It has been moved to a later date.
8	We need to cut back on the amount we spend on taxis and flights.	H	I'll let you know this afternoon.

Need help? → **Student's Book** page 187

Write a word or words for each definition. The first letter should help you.

1 A kind of training session which includes activities. **w**<u>orkshop</u>

2 The person with the same position in another company or country. **c**_____

3 A field of work which involves placing people in jobs. **r**_____

4 Give up a job or position, especially an important one. **s**_____ **d**_____

5 The amount of money taken by a business in a particular period. **t**_____

6 A person who is addicted to work. **w**_____

7 Another word for getting sacked. **d**_____

8 The amount of work that needs to be done. **w**_____

LISTENING PART 2

[QR code]

⊕ STRATEGY

- Read the sentences and <u>underline</u> the key words.
- Predict what type of words are missing.
- Remember you can write numbers.
- Read your sentences when you have finished. Are they grammatically correct?

🔊 24 You will hear a woman called Maya talking about her job as a florist. For questions 1–10, complete the sentences with a word or short phrase.

1 Maya originally studied __childcare__ .

2 Maya was employed by others for eight years before setting up her own _____ .

3 Maya says she was fortunate because her _____ provided a place for her to run her business.

4 Some people buy flowers to give to someone who is _____ from the workplace.

5 Maya is particularly happy when she does flowers for couples who are celebrating their _____ wedding anniversaries.

6 Maya explains that it can sometimes be difficult to arrange flowers for _____ because they have very high expectations.

7 The floristry trade has been impacted by changes to the _____ .

8 Maya's opinion is that everyone can be _____ if they try hard enough.

9 Maya says that florists should be _____ as some of their customers are buying flowers to say sorry to someone.

10 Florists have to compete with _____ for business.

➔ 🔊 Go to page 110 to read the audioscript if you need further help.

For more help with Listening Part 2:
➔ **Student's Book Exam Focus** page 103

WRITING PART 2: LETTER OF APPLICATION

1 **Read the Writing Part 2 task and highlight the key points to cover.**

> **! STRATEGY**
>
> - Read the task carefully.
> - Highlight or underline the information you must include in your e-mail.
> - Read your work carefully.
> - Check for spelling mistakes.

You see this advert for volunteers to work on projects abroad.

Volunteer with Help Abroad

Would you like to use your holidays to develop your skills, experience a new culture and meet people from all over the world? If so, our volunteering opportunities overseas could be for you. Choose from working on a farm, helping to build a school or teaching English to children. We have opportunities in South America, Africa and Asia.

Apply by email to John Patton at johnp@helpabroad.co.uk, saying why you want to volunteer with Help Abroad. Please tell us the kind of work you are interested in, the skills and personal qualities you have that make you suitable, and your preferred location.

Write your letter.

Now read the email written by a student.

Complete the email with the correct words.

> environmentally available
> ~~interest~~ opportunity project
> skills architecture

● ● ● ◀ ▶   🔍 🏠

Dear Mr Patton,

I am writing to express my ___interest___ in volunteering for Help Abroad. I am committed to improving life for people in the developing world and your organisation would give me an excellent _____ to do that.

I am interested mainly in construction work. I have done some bricklaying with my uncle during my school holidays and he has taught me some basic building _____ . I am planning to study _____ at university from next October and have a special interest in _____ friendly design. I think this would make me a strong candidate for the school-building _____ .

I am a very practical kind of person who likes to take a hands-on approach to whatever I do. I am also physically fit, which I feel would help with the work I have chosen. I am willing to go to any location where my skills are needed. However, as a Spanish speaker, I might be of greatest use in South America.

I am _____ at any time to discuss this opportunity further.

Yours sincerely

Gonzalo Muñoz

2 **Look at the criteria for the writing exam.**

Match the criteria to the examiner comments.

> Content   Organisation   Communicative achievement   ~~Language~~

1	_Language_	• The candidate uses collocation appropriately (special interest, environmentally friendly, hands-on approach). • Topic-specific vocabulary is used (developing world, bricklaying, building skills, project). • There is a good range of sentence structure (relative clauses, modals, verb patterns).
2	_____	• The email begins and ends with appropriate conventions of formal writing (Dear Mr, I am writing to, I am available, Yours sincerely). • The email is appropriately formal throughout.
3	_____	• Linking expressions are used to good effect (also, however). The writing avoids repetition through referencing (this would make me) and paraphrase (construction work … the work I have chosen).
4	_____	• All parts of the email relate to the task; the candidate has clearly explained what type of work he wants to do and the skills and personal qualities he could bring to the project. • Paragraphs are well organised and begin in a variety of ways.

For more help with Writing Part 2: Email / Letter
➔ **Student's Book Writing bank** page 236

HOW WAS UNIT 14?

Gave it a go   ⌐⌐

Needed a bit of help   ⌐⌐

Getting there   ⌐⌐

Aced it!   ⌐⌐

AUDIOSCRIPT

STARTER
🎧 **Track 02**

Speaker 1

I started learning English at school in my country and most people didn't take it very seriously at all. We had a lot of difficult academic subjects such as maths and science, so the English lessons were seen as a chance to relax a bit. The teacher was a young American guy. He was really nice but not strict like our other teachers. He got us to do role plays, which I thought would be a great opportunity for us to practise speaking. The trouble was, most of the time I was paired with a student who wouldn't try to speak English and either spoke in our language or didn't bother to do the activity at all.

Speaker 2

In my country we focused a lot on reading and grammar in our English lessons. We were encouraged to make sure we had chosen the correct tense and that the subject always agreed with the verb. Spelling was also considered very important. When I first came to the UK, I was terrified of opening my mouth and speaking English in case I made a grammatical mistake. It took several weeks before I would even say a few words. I was amazed that no one laughed at me. In fact, everyone helped me express myself and cared more about what I had to say than whether I made a mistake.

Speaker 3

I used to be very dependent on my translation app on my phone. It translates between English and my language. It took me a while to realise that people often didn't understand what I was saying or writing because I wasn't using natural English but a kind of weird computer translation. I'll still use it to look up words but I also use an English learners' dictionary to make sure I'm using the word or phrase correctly. I ask native speakers for feedback too – I've learned you have to use lots of different approaches when learning a language.

Speaker 4

When I decided to come to London, I spent a couple of months listening to British English speakers on the BBC news and in films and documentaries. By the time I arrived, I was able to understand the English accent easily. When I got to London, though, I was in for a shock! The reality was that in London people come from all over the world and from different parts of the UK. The skill I actually needed to develop was understanding a wide range of accents – even understanding people whose English was not as good as mine.

Speaker 5

In my country we learn American English, so when I came to the UK there were lots of things I noticed that were different. My teacher here said that it was OK to use either variety but we should be consistent. The problem was I got so confused. I knew the back of a car was a 'boot' or a 'trunk', but which was American and which was British? It was just so hard to remember. Now I speak a strange mix of American and British English!

🎧 **Track 03**

Speaker 1

Last weekend, we went to a music festival in another town. I'm usually the one in our group who organises stuff like that, so I got the tickets and booked a hostel for us to stay the night. There were eight of us altogether and we had a great time.

Speaker 2

I'd have to say my dad. We look alike, for a start. Also, we're both very ambitious and always looking out for the next opportunity. He started his career with a market stall when he was still in his teens and now he's got a whole chain of shops. He never stops working. I'm also very restless and always want to do something new.

Speaker 3

The best thing about my town is that you can be who you want to be there. People mind their own business and aren't interested in gossip. They're not bothered if you want to dress differently or dye your hair pink. I couldn't live somewhere where people judge you.

Speaker 4

I've always wanted to have a go at polo – you know that game you play on horseback with a ball and a stick called a hammer. I've been riding horses for years but I've never played polo, only watched it. You need a special kind of horse and other equipment so I'm not sure if I'll ever get the chance.

Speaker 5

Definitely my grandmother. She's such a character, so full of life, even though she's in her 80s now. You almost never find her at home, and she still walks everywhere. Her clothes are always fashionable and her hair's always nicely done. I hope I'm like her when I'm her age.

Speaker 6

Yes, when I was a kid I had a huge collection of badges. Some of them were from tourist places and others had slogans on them. Lots of them were of pop and rock bands. I used to pin them onto these big cotton sunhats. The hats were too heavy to wear but I hung them on hooks in my bedroom so everyone could see them.

Speaker 7

Most of my friends are still students so we try to find activities that don't cost us a lot of money. We've all got bicycles so we often go on long cycle rides and take a picnic with us. In my country, we have free entry to museums and art galleries so we often visit those places – or just hang out in the park.

Speaker 8

I've lived in my hometown ever since I was born. My parents and grandparents were all born here too, so we go back several generations. We're a well-known family in the town and I always see someone I know when I'm out.

UNIT 2

🔊 Track 04

Katie: So, how are you enjoying working life, Patrick?

Patrick: Umm, well, it has its ups and downs. I'm still getting used to it, to be honest. How about you?

Katie: Well, I've certainly found it easy to get used to having money to spend! Do you remember how we used to share a coffee because we couldn't afford one each?

Patrick: Yes, I do, and how we used to queue for hours to get cheap tickets for the theatre.

Katie: I know, happy days, eh? But we didn't use to get up very early, did we? I hardly ever used to make it to early lectures.

Patrick: Me neither, but I think I'm used to the early starts now. I've been working a few months longer than you, remember.

Katie: Well, I'm not used to the early mornings yet. I've been late a few times already. And I'm not used to having to dress smartly either. I miss my comfortable tracksuit trousers and T-shirts.

Patrick: Yeah, I know. I used to love going to uni in my pyjamas. No one cared how you looked. I still can't get used to wearing a tie every day!

🔊 Track 05

Interviewer: So, today we're talking about the ways the order in which children in a family are born affects each child's developing personality. Our guest is Dr Antonia Russo, a psychologist who has studied this area for several years. Good morning, Dr Russo. Tell us, how did you first become interested in the effects of birth order on personality?

Antonia Russo: Good morning and thanks for inviting me. This whole topic has interested me since childhood. I'm a middle child myself and I made the conscious decision to have only two children because I always felt like the odd one out as a child, which, admittedly, I found both fascinating and strange at the same time. When I became a psychologist, I was keen to find out whether there was any evidence to support how I felt as a middle child and whether this was the same for other families.

Interviewer: You argue that the firstborn children are often more successful than their siblings. Why is this?

AR: Well, the oldest child tends to be quite controlling and they are typically diligent high achievers. Furthermore, it's natural for first-time parents to be more attentive. They often encourage their firstborns to try out many different activities, such as sports and music, which means that firstborn children are more likely to discover their gifts and talents. They are also more likely to be CEOs of companies, and that often comes from the fact that they learn to manage people, i.e. their younger brothers and sisters as they grow up.

Interviewer: That's really interesting. I'm the baby of my family, so what can you tell us about the characteristics of the youngest child?

AR: Well, the good thing is they are likely to be uncomplicated, meaning that they are clear about who they are and what their role is. Compare that to, say, their older siblings, who often don't know this and can suffer from a crisis of confidence. The youngest is known to be outgoing and fun-loving. Being the 'cute' younger one, they probably realised that they are more likely to get what they want and that gave them confidence. That being said, they are often accused of being self-centred as a result of this.

Interviewer: That sounds like me! But you're a middle child. How do you think this influenced you growing up?

AR: Well, I was born between two sisters and we didn't always see eye to eye, to be honest. My elder sister had the chance to do more things and my younger sister was a typical youngest child. I had to find my own way of standing out from the crowd – and like many middle children, I did that outside the family. I developed a huge circle of friends and didn't always do what my parents told me to do – that was my way of getting noticed, I suppose.

Interviewer: And, of course, we mustn't forget to mention only children. What are they like?

AR: Well, they tend to mature quite quickly and often value their privacy more than, say, those who grow up with brothers and sisters. This is usually because they spend more time on their own. However, there is no evidence to suggest that they are more spoilt; in fact, the opposite is true in most cases. When researching only children, I found that they have more in common with the oldest child, in that they both tend to make good leaders. But I should also say that the evidence points to oldest children being more successful as heads of companies, even countries, than only children.

Interviewer: I see. Do you think that gender plays a role in how children develop?

AR: That's an interesting question. There are psychologists who believe that gender plays a vital role in the development of children's personalities and that it's something that should be researched further. I do sometimes question whether or not this is accurate, though, as none of the research I've come across suggests that it has a big influence on children's personalities as they grow up. Furthermore, I don't think that it's something that the mother and father need to think about too seriously in terms of personality development when it comes to bringing up their children.

Interviewer: That's interesting to know. So, in conclusion, how would you summarise your findings?

AR: Well, there have been enough studies to show that birth order matters and that there are definitely tendencies for oldest, youngest, middle and only children to have certain personality types. However, when you're dealing with humans, it's not as simple as saying 'all firstborn children are like this'. Birth order is just one influence on a child's personality. Genetics, experience in and indeed outside the family, culture and environment all play a part too – so it's not a straightforward subject.

Interviewer: Thank you, Dr Russo.

UNIT 3
🎧 **Track 06**

Donny: So, Ms Poulter, what advice would you give me regarding my plans to study medicine?

Teacher: Well, to start with, you might like to visit a few practising doctors to find out what working in a hospital is actually like. It's not as glamorous as many people think. And why not try to get some work experience so you can find out if it's really for you? I'd probably consider volunteering at a few charities or nursing homes just to get a taste of what working in healthcare is like.

Oh, and make sure you find other like-minded students to share your ideas with. For example, I'd recommend joining a few web forums where actual medical students share their experiences. Talking to somebody with similar plans or experience can be really helpful.

What else? Well, you should start reading up on the different medical specialities now. It can be a good idea to think about which areas you are actually interested in – or at least to rule out any that you definitely don't want to do. I'd suggest having a list of two or three possible specialities.

Some people pin all their hopes on one specific medical career and then find it difficult to get on the course they need. Having more than one possibility means you do have an alternative if you don't get the grades you need.

Last but not least, you'd better start going to university open days soon. That's essential not only to check that a course is right for you, but also to find a place you would be happy to live and study in. I have ex-students who accepted places on courses before seeing the facilities and meeting the lecturers – they discovered only after they'd started that the course was not what they were looking for. So be careful!

🎧 **Track 07**

Examiner: Now I'd like you to talk together about something for about two minutes. Here are some factors that students must consider when choosing a university to study at. Talk to each other about why these might be important to students.

Mario: OK, Yuriko, where shall we start? What do you think is the most important factor?

Yuriko: Umm, well, they're all important but let's talk about the reputation or rankings first. Some people are really obsessed with what's said about the university or what its position in the rankings is.

Mario: Sorry, but can you explain what the rankings are? I've never heard that term before.

Yuriko: Yes, it means lists of universities from best to worst published by newspapers. They change every year, but in the UK, the universities of Oxford and Cambridge are always at the top.

Mario: Oh, I see. Well, I'd say it's not as important as all that. I mean, who decides on those positions anyway?

Yuriko: I'm afraid I completely disagree with you there. After all, that university will be on your CV for the rest of your life. What I mean by that is that it's really crucial to go to the best university you possibly can. Most employers will use the rankings to judge the quality of an applicant's degree.

Mario: Well, I suppose you might be right, but to be honest, I'm not convinced that's the case. OK, let's talk about location. Do most people consider that, do you think?

Yuriko: I think it varies a lot from person to person. Some students need to find a university near to where they live, don't they? But lots of people move to a different country to get a better education, so that's a tricky one.

Mario: Yes, I'd go along with that. I couldn't wait to get away from my hometown, but some of my friends went to the university nearest home. So, shall we think about cost now?

Yuriko: Well, this has to be a major factor, doesn't it? If you can't afford the fees, you can't go!

Mario: I'm not so sure about that. You can always get a student loan to pay for your course and pay it back once you're working. And don't all universities cost the same in terms of study fees?

Yuriko: Not necessarily – they do vary a bit – but I see your point. OK, moving on, I'd say that facilities are a huge consideration for students, aren't they?

Mario: I couldn't agree more, particularly if you want to do a scientific subject or perhaps engineering. I think that's probably the most important thing to consider for those students. What do you think?

Yuriko: Yes, you're right, though it's possibly less important for arts students.

Mario: That's true. So, the last point is job opportunities. Do you know what they mean by that?

Yuriko: Yes, I think so. We're talking about the rankings again. They collect information about how many graduates of each university get jobs, how soon they get jobs and how much they get paid. You can check the rankings for that too.

Mario: That's the most important of all, then!

Yuriko: Well, I agree up to a point, but there is a lot of information those figures can't show us. I mean, do the students get jobs they like, are they happy in those workplaces and how soon do they get pay rises?

Examiner: Thank you. Now you have a minute to decide which of the factors …

🔺 **Track 08**

Examiner: Thank you. Now you have a minute to decide which of the factors would be most important for younger students.

Mario: OK. All of them are important so it's going to be hard to decide. Perhaps we can rule some out. For a start, I would say that location is not going to be important for everybody. What do you think?

Yuriko: Yes, you're right. And I think you were right about cost, too. Course fees are generally the same for all universities in the UK, so that's not likely to be a major consideration when choosing one university over another. I mean, it costs more or less the same wherever you go.

Mario: Agreed. I think we need to consider why students go to university. For me, the main reason is to get a good job afterwards, right? Surely job opportunities has to be the main motivating factor.

Yuriko: For many yes, but for other students it's the academic side of things that matters. The reputation of the university, the standard of its lecturers and how good its facilities are – you know, that sort of thing.

Mario: I'm not convinced that's the most important thing for the majority of students, at least in my country, but I can see your point. Ultimately, I think it depends on the needs of the individual. So I'm going to stick with job opportunities as my number one.

Yuriko: OK, in that case, I'm going to choose something related to that – such as reputation. As I said earlier, employers look at your university when they assess you as a potential employee. The right university can lead to the right job.

Examiner: Thank you.

UNIT 4
🔘 **Track 09**

1

Getting down to where my parents live was an absolute nightmare. It's actually not that far, but there were problems on the track and we were delayed for about an hour getting out of the city. After about 20 minutes, we just stopped. We weren't at a station and we didn't get any information about what was happening. We just sat there for over half an hour wondering what was going on. Luckily, there was someone serving sandwiches and drinks. They were expensive but at least we had something to eat.

2

Man: Did you get a supersaver ticket? It's a lot cheaper if you're doing more than one journey.

Woman: Yes, it works out as quite reasonable, doesn't it? I've tried to avoid taking the train since the fares went up so much.

Man: I know what you mean, but this bus isn't doing my back any good. The driver seems to be in a bit of a rush.

Woman: A bit? I think he must be running late – and these new buses have such hard seats.

Man: Yeah, they could do with being a bit softer, couldn't they?

3

Man: I can't believe we actually saw the Sunflowers!

Woman: You know it's not the only version of it, don't you? There are at least three others.

Man: I know, but this was the first one I've seen. I loved it, but I'm not so keen on the artist's dark period. Did you see the one of the woman digging in the field? It was so gloomy.

Woman: Yes, but he had a lot of talent. Anyway, I'm tired after all that walking. How about having a look in the gift shop to see if we can find some presents for Oliver and Sophie?

4

So, your holiday is all booked for you. Seven nights at the Blue Sapphire resort in Santorini. The price includes the three excursions you selected so you don't have to worry about that. Oh, before I forget, as you're going in January and the nights can get a bit chilly, remember to pack a jumper or jacket. OK, the excursions all include a pick-up from the hotel and they're included in the insurance you've purchased with the package. So if they're cancelled for any reason, you'll get a full refund.

5

Last night Julie, my daughter, wanted me to watch that Holiday programme she likes so much. Usually, that's not really my kind of thing as I don't especially want to listen to endless advice about places I'll probably never go to. Anyway, this episode was about Bangkok. I didn't think it would be that good, but it was absolutely brilliant. The street food looks amazing and there's a market that goes on till the early hours of the morning. I still wouldn't go there, though, because it's a 15-hour flight and over 30 degrees most of the year.

6

The last time we had a long weekend we went to a town called Bewdley, which is near Birmingham. It has these little winding lanes with cute country cottages which all looked similar to each other. I felt like I'd gone back in time and was about 10 years old again – I'm not sure if I've told you but I grew up in a village with a river running through it just like Bewdley. So that was nice, but Amy and Ben didn't enjoy it that much as there's not a lot for kids to do there.

7

Hi. We're thinking of booking a stay at your hotel. I've already checked your website and the room we want is available for our dates. I just have a few questions before we make a final decision. We're coming with our children – who are four and two – so I was wondering whether I need to hire a car. It all depends on whether the public transport is reliable and taxis are easy to get hold of. We're hoping to go out to restaurants in the nearby villages most evenings and we need to be sure we can get there and back easily with the kids.

8

Well, I did enjoy the cruise most of the time but to be honest, I wouldn't go again. It was great to see the scenery from the ship and the places we saw weren't as bad as I'd expected. But the thing about a cruise, though, is that you're stuck on board for days at a time with the same group of people. They only had one band and they kept playing the same old songs. We ate in the restaurant every night. I suppose I can't really complain about the food and it was good that it was included in the price of the trip. But we had to pay for everything else.

🔊 Track 10

Speaker 1

Krakavany is a small village about an hour's drive from Prague, the capital of the Czech Republic. It's a sleepy little place, with just one shop, a school and not much else really. It's surrounded by pine forests. There's no water close by, no lakes or rivers, so many people have swimming pools in their gardens because it's absolutely boiling in summer. It's such a peaceful place but it's not very exciting.

Speaker 2

I haven't passed my driving test yet so I usually take the bus or tram to school. Sometimes I get a lift from one of my friends as a few of them have got driving licences already. In the summer I might walk if I've got the energy, but that's not very often!

Speaker 3

It depends on the season. If it's the summer holidays, I spend a lot of time at the beach with my friends. We play beach volleyball and sometimes have barbecues in the evenings. During the winter holidays, we just hang out at each other's houses or go out for pizza or something like that.

Speaker 4

I'd probably choose a city break as I live in the countryside and big cities are much more exciting. I particularly like cities where there's great nightlife and also cultural attractions such as museums and art galleries. I'd definitely want to stay right in the centre, where all the action is.

UNIT 6

🔊 Track 11

Speaker 1

A few years ago, I volunteered at a local animal sanctuary. The project involved looking after the monkeys they had there. I know a few people were really irritated by the co-ordinator leading the project, who they felt was quite rude and distant at times. Personally, I didn't have a problem with him and we got along quite well. In fact, at the end of the programme, he told me that he was really proud of the work I'd done. This gave me the confidence to apply for a full-time job at the animal sanctuary and I've been working there ever since.

Speaker 2

I have just finished a six-week volunteer programme at the local wildlife park. The people working at the park were really good, despite the lack of support they received from the local council in terms of funding, which is why they were looking for volunteers in the first place. They taught us everything we needed to know to do the job properly, which I really respected as they didn't have a lot of free time themselves. I thought it would be quite boring, you know, doing the same things every day, but I actually really enjoyed the work I did there.

Speaker 3

I'd never considered becoming a volunteer until a friend of mine told me about how rewarding and inspiring it was for her when she did it. I love nature and so I applied for a programme that looked after the local wildlife at a nature reserve. I remember on my first day when they asked me to feed one of the horses and I ended up feeding the wrong one, which I still can't believe I did! I was relieved, though, when my mentor told me that this wasn't such a big deal and that it actually happened all the time.

Speaker 4

I volunteered as an assistant at the natural history museum last month. I thought it would be a really good opportunity to get experience as I'm currently studying biology at university. I can't complain about the organisation because they were able to accommodate me at quite short notice. The majority of the people who worked there were really friendly, except for my boss, who wasn't really that interested in teaching me anything. That was quite irritating as that was the main reason why I wanted to work there in the first place.

Speaker 5

During the school holidays, I went to work for the local aquarium. I was only allowed to work there for a week, which was a little annoying as I wanted to spend the whole summer there. The person who looked after me was really nice. She kept calling me by the wrong name on the first day, which she was really embarrassed about when I corrected her at the end of the day. I didn't mind, though. We did a lot during that week and by the end I was really impressed with what I'd accomplished in such a short space of time.

UNIT 7

🔊 Track 12

Sofia: OK, so I think it would be really nice to have a formal dinner at a restaurant. What do you think?

Enrique: Well, I agree it would be nice, but I don't think many of the students were planning to spend a lot on the party.

Sofia: You've got a point. It would be quite expensive. So what about going for a pizza?

Enrique: Yes, I think that would work well. There's that Italian restaurant just around the corner. It's cheap and pretty convenient.

Sofia: That's true and their pizzas are delicious. So that's a possibility. What about everyone cooking a dish at home? We could all make something from our different countries. That would be really fun.

Enrique: Definitely not! I can't cook at all and neither can a lot of the students.

Sofia: Oh, come on! There must be something simple you can make. It might turn out better than you think.

Enrique: No, really. It won't work. Maybe we should have tea, coffee and cake. If the party is straight after school, it will be 4.30 and that's what people usually eat at that time.

Sofia: Well, yes, but it's not very special, is it? We have coffee and cake almost every day, don't we?

Enrique: I suppose so. So that leaves the snacks, then. Personally, I'm not keen on this option because it's so unhealthy. When there are crisps and nuts, I just can't stop eating!

Sofia: I know what you mean. All right, then. I think there's only one option we both like, isn't there? I hope the rest of the class will be happy with that.

🔊 Track 13

Speaker 1
There are a lot of special foods we prepare for festivals in my country. For the most important festival, we make biriyani, usually with chicken or lamb. The main ingredient is rice, plus lots of different spices. It takes quite a long time to make, which is why it's really tasty. We serve it with yoghurt and pickles.

Speaker 2
Nowadays, like most families in my country, we don't sit and eat a meal together every day because everyone is busy with work and extra classes. But on Sundays, we always get together at my grandparents' house and have a huge meal. My grandma is an amazing cook and my aunts and uncles usually bring cakes and desserts, so I always enjoy Sunday lunch.

Speaker 3
Indian cuisine is extremely popular. The food is really tasty and filling and you can ask them to make it less spicy if you want. It's ideal for vegetarians like me as all the food is clearly separated into vegetables or meat. Most Indian restaurants are very good value for money as they give large portions, and they often do home delivery too.

Speaker 4
A few weeks ago, we had a party for my grandparents' golden wedding anniversary. It was at an Italian restaurant called Franco's. There were so many different dishes to choose from. I had garlic mushrooms as a starter and salmon for the main course. There were huge dishes of pasta and salads on the tables. The desserts were amazing, too. I ate so much that I was absolutely stuffed!

UNIT 8
🔊 Track 14

Speaker 1
I have used them before but I don't really know how to do calculations or anything like that. If someone else has set one up, I can add data into the rows and columns, but I don't know any of the formulas.

Speaker 2
I've only recently found out how to do this. On my device you have to press the home button and the sleep/wake button at the same time. You hear a click and it's saved to photos. I think it's a bit different on laptops and PCs though.

Speaker 3

Nowadays it happens automatically on some devices, but if that doesn't apply to yours, you'll have to save everything to a hard drive or the cloud or you'll lose all your work if your device stops working.

Speaker 4

Well, the whole point of them is that it's really easy to find what you're looking for on your computer screen. The symbols are quite colourful and clear so you can easily see where each programme is, or what kind of file you have.

Speaker 5

These relate to either hardware or software. Obviously with software they happen much more regularly, so with some programmes it could be every few weeks. They are generally free, quick and easy. With hardware, you have to buy new equipment, so it can be difficult and expensive.

Speaker 6

These don't happen very often – only a couple of times a century, most probably. It's when something is developed or discovered that really moves science or technology forward – things such as the invention of 3D printing or the development of certain medicines.

🔘 Track 15

Good evening. I'm here tonight to talk about my work as a marine biologist and, more specifically, my work with seahorse conservation. I'll start by telling you something about these adorable little creatures and, before I finish, I'll tell you what you can do to help protect them.

Some of you may know that seahorses are the only species in which the male gives birth. The female passes the eggs to the male and he grows the babies. It only takes two to six weeks, though. He gives birth to hundreds at a time. Before you start wondering why we haven't been taken over by seahorses, I should point out that only around one in 20 of these babies survive. Sadly, many of them are eaten by predators.

Seahorses mate for life, but the males and females live in separate territories. Every morning they meet up with their partner. They actually change colour when they see each other and do a kind of dance display, which can last up to an hour.

Something else that has always interested me about seahorses is that they have to eat constantly. They need to consume up to 3,000 pieces of food every day. This is because they don't have a stomach. They suck up their food with their long, straw-like mouths – or snouts – rather like an elephant. They can't chew so the food disintegrates as they eat. Their snouts can expand to allow them to take larger prey.

Seahorses live all over the world and there are over 40 different species. The smallest are the size of your little fingernail and the biggest could be larger than your hand. All types of seahorses have wonderful eyesight. In fact, their eyes can move independently so that they can keep an eye out for all the food they need. To swim they beat their dorsal fin – the fin on their backs – between 30 and 70 times per second! Their tails are also really cool because they can use them to grip hold of things. But, unfortunately, seahorses are extremely delicate creatures. They can easily be damaged or even killed. Because they are so fascinating, people try to capture them on film, but a camera flash can be very harmful to them.

Now, because seahorses are such unique creatures, there are lots of myths and cultural beliefs about them around the world. For example, it is believed that eating seahorses can make you strong. Also, seahorses are used in traditional medicine and are very much in demand – both dead and alive – as souvenirs and for aquarium displays. Every year between 15 and 20 million seahorses are caught and traded around the world. We don't realistically believe that we will be able to put a stop to that completely, but the seahorse population needs to be sustainable. In my conservation organisation, we're working at many different levels to protect seahorses in their natural habitats. One of the things we do is work with governments to place restrictions on catching and trading seahorses. We work with local populations to set up 'no take' areas, where seahorses can live undisturbed.

There are several ways in which you can help. First of all, you can record your seahorse sightings and upload them to our website so that we can learn more about where seahorses are and in what kind of numbers and condition. Also, you can adopt a seahorse. No, you can't take it home, but your donation will help us conserve these wonderful little creatures.

UNIT 9
🎧 Track 16

Honza, Czech Republic
OK, a place I've visited in my country is called Kutná Hora. It's a town on the banks of the River Vrchlice. There are loads of historic buildings, such as the Cathedral of St Barbara, which is really stunning. Actually, I would say it's just as beautiful as Prague. In some ways the atmosphere is even better because there are fewer tourists and it's more relaxed. If you get the chance, I'd definitely recommend a visit.

Alicia, Spain
One really memorable place I've visited in Spain is Ciudad Encantada. The name means Enchanted City and it really is the most breathtaking place I've ever seen. Over many years, the rocks have been formed into strange shapes by the weather and the water from the nearby river. Many of the rocks have imaginative names – for example, Mushroom Rock, the Turtle, the Bears and so on. When I went there, it was a misty day and the atmosphere was really mysterious. We lit a campfire and told each other scary stories. It was a lot of fun! Everyone should go there.

UNIT 10
🎧 Track 17

Jan
I think it would be a good idea to introduce a four-day working week. I know that in comparison with the past we have a lot of leisure time, but there are several reasons why it is still not enough. First of all, life in general is a lot busier than it was. What I feel is that technology has actually given us more to do. For example, we have to update our social media, answer emails and keep up with all the latest TV shows just so that we can talk to our friends about them. There's a lot of pressure on young people in particular. We have to know about the latest songs and movies and keep up with fashion. Most of us don't have time to work five days a week!

Isabel
On balance, I feel that most of us have about the right amount of leisure time. The majority of us work or study for more or less eight hours a day, which gives us eight hours to sleep and another eight to do household chores, meet friends and relax. Besides, for most of us work is not as hard as it was in the past because we have machines to help us. This means we are not as tired at the end of the day. Having said that, lots of people have to move far away from their hometown for work or college, so sometimes a two-day weekend is not enough to go back and spend time with family and friends. But in my view, we don't need a three-day weekend every week – just a few more each year.

Track 18

Speaker 1

I started diving when I was on holiday in Thailand about six years ago. I'd always wanted to have a go and even thought about doing it professionally. There are lots of jobs that involve scuba diving but you need a much higher level of training. I've done a basic course, which allows you to dive to a depth of 40 metres. It's true you need a lot of equipment, but most people hire it. Even for recreational diving, you do have to be quite fit, but diving as a hobby is not nearly as risky as people think.

Speaker 2

I started gymnastics at the age of four. It's best to start young as children are very flexible before they turn five. Although female gymnasts tend to be short and slim, they are extremely strong. You also need to be a risk-taker because injury is always a possibility. There are lots of different kinds of apparatus, such as parallel bars, rings and the balance beam. You also have floor exercises, which use balls, hoops and ribbons. Some equipment is used only by men, some only by women and some by both. For me it's just a hobby – being a professional gymnast must be a lot of work!

Speaker 3

I've been taking part in equestrian events since I was about 12. I have my own horse, a grey called Monty, who I keep at the local riding stables. The cost of keeping him there is lower because the school uses him for lessons. A few years ago, I started taking part in tournaments. You get showing classes, where you just walk, trot and canter around the ring, or jumping contests. I feel that people get too competitive in this sport. Although Monty and I have won lots of prizes, I don't really care if we win or lose. I just enjoy taking part.

Speaker 4

I learned to play chess at school. You have to concentrate really hard and plan a lot of moves ahead. There are different pieces such as the king, the queen and the knights. All of them have their own way of moving – but that's the easy part. The hard part is planning your moves so that your opponent's king gets into trouble and can't be saved. I've taken part in a few tournaments but I've never won one. The winners are people who can dedicate many hours every day to chess. I'm too busy with schoolwork for that.

Speaker 5

I've got quite a good collection now – maybe 200 or more in total, so it's not a cheap hobby. The craze for action figures started in the 1960s, but really took off in the 80s. The most popular ones are Transformers, Star Wars and the heroes from the Marvel comics. My favourites are Power Rangers and I have about 20 or 30 different ones. Most action figures are between seven and 28 centimetres tall but my biggest, Galactus, is five times larger than average. I sometimes swap figures with my friends. We all know which ones are rare and worth more. It's really exciting when you find an unusual one.

Track 19

Christina: OK, so shall we discuss the cinema complex first? Do you think it's a good idea?

Todd: Well, I absolutely love going to see films but, to be honest, I feel that people don't go to the cinema much any more, in comparison to, say, when our parents were young.

Christina: I know, most people watch films online so I'm not sure if it's worth building a complete new cinema. I mean, we already have a cinema in this town.

Todd: OK, let's come back to that one. What about a bowling centre? We don't have bowling yet, do we?

Christina: No, but don't you think it would only be for young people? I don't think older people would go there. We should probably choose something that everyone can enjoy.

Todd: In that case, the community park is the best idea. There could be things older people like, such as a rose garden and tea rooms, as well as a park for kids to play in.

Christina: Yes, and one of those outdoor gyms which all ages can use to keep fit.

Todd: Those are brilliant. The cost of gym membership is too high for retired people and students. Being outside is much healthier anyway.

Christina: I think it might be one of the cheapest options as well. So, are we still considering the cinema?

Todd: No, the community park is by far the best option.

UNIT 12
🔊 Track 20

Interviewer: Today we're talking to Paul Fenton, who's an independent film festival organiser. Welcome, Paul. That sounds like an interesting job. Can you tell us how you got into it?

Paul Fenton: Well, a lot of people are surprised that such a job exists, and to be honest, it hasn't existed for all that long. Until about 20 years ago, there were only a few well-known national and international film festivals, but in recent years, the number of people interested in unusual films has really increased and a greater number of film festivals focus on specific interests.

Interviewer: Is the Brief Encounters festival in Bristol an example of this?

PF: Yes, absolutely. Whereas in the past a festival might be named after its geographical location – the Chichester Film Festival, for example – now they are more likely to be based on one genre or a type of movie. Brief Encounters is a good example because it screens only short films. A festival might just show films related to immigration or the environment, for instance. Those are very hot topics at the moment.

Interviewer: How should people decide what kind of festival to hold?

PF: Before you decide on a theme or genre, you need to do a lot of research about what's already available in the local area and what people want, how far they would be prepared to travel and how much money they have to spend. Otherwise, a festival is unlikely to last long. One of the things I do is advise people on the market for different types of film, particularly if they are hoping to start a festival that will become an annual event.

Interviewer: Why else might a festival end?

PF: One example is The Fantasm festival of horror, sci-fi and fantasy, which took place in London until the late 1990s. It had to stop because it ran out of films to show. The theme just wasn't broad enough.. The Sheffield International Documentary Festival, for example, is more sustainable as there will always be a ready supply of new documentaries.

Interviewer: I see. And what other aspects of organising a film festival do people run into difficulties with?

PF: The primary problem I deal with is that organisers often underestimate the time needed to plan a successful festival. Almost everyone who tries this for the first time misunderstands what's involved in terms of work. That's why there is a need for someone like me to come in from the very beginning and help with the organisation. Most people seem to think it'll take three to six months at most, but that's just not realistic – you need to realise it will take at least a year to get ready.

Interviewer: What else do they need guidance with?

PF: In my experience, almost everything! Once you've decided what to show, it's important to make sure that the films are available on the dates you've planned. I can help here with legal and copyright issues – new organisers are often not aware of these. Then you need to make sure the venues are the right size and that you have a publicity campaign in place so that people know about the festival. I've got a lot of experience with these too.

Interviewer: So, it's a lot of work planning a festival?

PF: Yes, it is! Anyone putting on a festival will need to hire administrative staff and a capable manager. You'll need marketing staff who know your local area well and are familiar with online marketing, too. Ideally, you'll be able to attract media students as volunteers. There are so many issues to consider, including national regulations on film certification and getting a licence to show films from your local authority. My job is to advise my clients on all aspects of the festival and make sure they don't miss anything.

UNIT 13

🔊 Track 21

Marc: So, what do you want to do today? Shall we go into town?

Julia: Yeah, OK, we could maybe do a little window shopping.

Marc: Actually, I was thinking of hunting out a few bargains.

Julia: Umm, I know all about your bargains. With you, a little look around the shops always turns into a shopping spree!

Marc: Not this time. I'm on a very tight budget at the moment.

Julia: That's what you say, but I know how you love your designer brands.

Marc: You can pick up good brands at reasonable prices if you're willing to shop around a bit.

Julia: Well, I'm sure you're not going to come home empty-handed.

Marc: Maybe not, but I'm not going to overspend like I did last time.

Julia: We'll see about that.

🔊 Track 22

Hamid

Umm, well, both women are shopping in markets. I think they are both enjoying themselves because they don't appear to be in a hurry at all. In fact, they look very relaxed. In the first picture, the lady is choosing some food – it looks like fruit. There are so many different types to choose from. That's probably one reason why she's enjoying it. Also, I think the food looks very fresh – it might be locally grown and organic. I can see other shoppers in the background. The woman in the second photo is at a different kind of market. The things on sale seem to be secondhand or could be antiques. In this kind of market, you can pick up unique items at bargain prices, so that might be why she looks happy. Both these photos show nice, relaxing places to shop.

UNIT 14

🔊 **Track 23**

Speaker 1

The job has changed quite a bit over the 10 years I've been doing it. I used to spend most of my time at the back of the shop, packing up medicines and printing the labels – things like that. But now that it's much harder to get an appointment with a doctor, a lot of people ask me to suggest something they should take. They show me their injuries or describe their symptoms to me. It's a lot more interesting now.

Speaker 2

I'm self-employed, which suits me because I'd get really bored just going to one workplace and doing the same thing every day. I'm based at home, but I'm always out and about meeting clients and working on projects. I advise people who are trying to start up their own businesses – I help out with the marketing, websites and anything related to business start-ups.

Speaker 3

It started as a hobby, but now I do it full-time. The first place I bought was a run-down cottage just outside the city. I started working on it at the weekends and found I had a real talent for making houses look great inside and out. Surprisingly, the area suddenly became popular and I made a huge profit when I sold the cottage. I used that money to buy an old warehouse down by the river – which I converted into luxury flats. It's great to have a job I love so much.

Speaker 4

In my current post, I'm working with personal clients – people who have made or inherited large sums of money. I give them advice on the law relating to the payment of taxes and, in particular, help them understand how they can pay as little as possible to the government within the law. Some people think this is a boring job, but it's actually really interesting because you meet different people and learn how they made their money and how they spend it. It's very satisfying when you save people money.

Speaker 5

What I like most about my job is that there's never a dull moment. You have to be alert because the situation in the skies above the airport is ever-changing. We have even more lives in our hands than pilots because we are directing a large number of planes at the same time. We have to make sure they are a safe distance apart and direct pilots to a runway for landing. I would hate a job where things get boring. There's a constant buzz in the control tower. It can get crazy but that's part of what I love about it.

Speaker 6

I usually do about five or six children's parties a week. That doesn't sound like much but believe me, there's a lot of work involved. Depending on the package the client has chosen, I have to choose my costumes and props and practise the show. I do magic tricks, juggling and mime, and I am also a 'one man band', which means I play several instruments at the same time. Kids nowadays are really smart and they get bored easily so I have to make sure there are lots of surprises.

🔊 **Track 24**

I didn't plan on becoming a florist. I was looking for a part-time job while I was at college doing a course in child care and my local florist had a Saturday vacancy advertised, so I thought I'd apply. At first I didn't have much interest in flowers but gradually I came to love the work. I learned so much from my first boss, Janet. She seemed to know exactly which flowers were needed for each occasion. I worked for Janet full-time for a couple of years and then for another florist for around six. After that, I felt ready to start up a business myself. I was lucky that my uncle had an empty property, which he rented to me for a very low rent so I found it easier than most to get started.

Being a florist is about so much more than just the flowers. Although some people come in and buy flowers because they love them, customers are usually buying them for a special occasion and they want them to be perfect. Most people end up having a chat about why they're buying the flowers – for a birthday or anniversary, or because a colleague of theirs is retiring from work, for example. If you are a people person, it's a great opportunity to meet people and find out about their lives. It's really lovely to do flowers for the birth of a baby or a golden wedding – imagine being married for 50 years! That's incredible and it gives me a lot of pleasure to help people celebrate these amazing events.

As you can imagine, weddings are one of our largest sources of business. Dealing with brides can be the most challenging part of the job because most of them have very specific – and not always practical – ideas about what they want. Often a woman will come in 18 months before her wedding day and say 'I must have this kind of flower in this colour', but what they don't understand is that it's impossible to predict what's going to be available a year and a half from now. One thing which has affected our business is global warming. The weather is a lot less predictable than it used to be, which means we can't say for sure what type of flower will be in season in a particular month. That makes it hard for people getting married. We always try to have a backup plan in case their first choice is not available.

There's a lot of creativity involved in deciding which colours and types of flower go together and arranging them in attractive ways. I didn't really think of myself as a creative person, but now I believe that anyone can be like that. But they have to put their mind to it. But florists also need to be sensitive. We sometimes have to deal with someone who's forgotten their husband's or wife's birthday or people who are sending flowers to make up with someone after an argument. Part of your job is to help customers choose the right flowers.

In the last few years we've diversified a little. We now sell gifts, such as chocolates, picture frames and teddy bears, as well as greetings cards and balloons. You have to move with the times. We face huge competition from supermarkets, but I think our personal, friendly approach is the key to our success.

ACKNOWLEDGEMENTS

The authors and publishers would like to thank: Phil Dexter, Inclusive Education Consultant, and Orsolya Misik-Szatzker, teacher specialising in language learning for dyslexic students, for their insights and expertise during the development process.

Lucy Passmore and Jishan Uddin for their contribution to the grammar animations.

The authors and publishers acknowledge the following sources of copyright material and are grateful for the permissions granted. While every effort has been made, it has not always been possible to identify the sources of all the material used, or to trace all copyright holders. If any omissions are brought to our notice, we will be happy to include the appropriate acknowledgements on reprinting and in the next update to the digital edition, as applicable.

Key: UST = Unit Starter, U = Unit

Text
U3: Portfolio School for the text about the school. Copyright © Portfolio School. Reproduced with kind permission.

Photography
All the images are sourced from Getty Images.

UST: Klaus Vedfelt/DigitalVision; SolStock/iStock/Getty Images Plus; Tony Anderson/Taxi; **U1:** Cultura RM Exclusive/Alan Graf; Felix Man/Stringer/Picture Post; Mike Harrington/DigitalVision; **U2:** Caiaimage/Robert Daly; FatCamera/E+; **U3:** Ariel Skelley/DigitalVision; Portra/DigitalVision; **U4:** Andrew TB Tan/Moment; levente bodo/Moment; Tais Policanti/Momen; **U5:** Tim Robberts/The Image Bank; Anthony Harvie/Stone; Ravindra Bhor/iStock/Getty Images Plus; Tetra Images; **U6:** Gary Vestal/Photographer's Choice; moodboard/Brand X Pictures; Chris Cheadle/All Canada Photos; **U7:** mikroman6/Moment; David Malan/Photographer's Choice; Mike Kemp; **U8:** Indeed; Dong Wenjie/Moment; Dennis Macdonald/Photographer's Choice RF; **U9:** Caiaimage/Sam Edwards; Hero Images; Vlad Fishman/Moment; Ventura Carmona/Moment; ; **U11:** Westend61; Mike Kemp/Blend Images; Caiaimage/Martin Barraud; **U12:** Gpointstudio/Image Source; NLink/iStock/Getty Images Plus; **U13:** JAG IMAGES/Cultura; Vostok/Moment; Hoxton/Tom Merton; asiseeit/E+; **U14:** kali9/E+; Alys Tomlinson/Cultura; Ariel Skelley/DigitalVision.

Front cover photography by Supawat Punnanon/EyeEm; Patrick Foto; fStop Images-Caspar Benson; art2002; Alexander Spatari; primeimages.

Illustrations
Derren Toussaint (In the style of Steven Johnson).

Animations
Grammar animation video production by QBS Learnings. Voiceover by Dan Strauss.

Audio
Produced by Creative Listening and recorded at Tileyard Studios, London.
Reading text audio produced by Dan Strauss.

Page make up
Blooberry Design